COLLECTED POEMS, 1941–2004

Collected Poems, 1941–2004

DIANA ROOSEVELT

Diana P. Reeve Literary Trust
Boston
2010

Diana P. Reeve Literary Trust
c/o Choate Hall and Stewart LLP
Two International Place
Boston, MA 02110

ISBN: 978-0-615-36040-9

Library of Congress Control Number: 2010903392

Printed in the United States of America

Contents

1   The Blue Rose

11   Icicle Butterfly Tree

35   The Egg

41   The Black Lily

71   The Rainbow Shell

79   Singing Beach

99   The Fountain

107   The Rose

115   The Alps

145   The Wheat

159   Swallow Hill

177   The Wild Swans in Pennsylvania

185   The Crimson Crocus

199   The Sun Path

213   Later Poems

233   A Contrast of Ice and Glass

243   The Valley

247   Index of First Lines

259   List of Poems with Titles

The Blue Rose

All gardens stifle one who looked
Once on your eyes' dark roses,
Though lids and leaves have fallen
And skull branch whitens bare.

All summers stifle one who gazed
Once at your eyes' dark ocean,
Though storming waves have fallen
To still seas, open air.

Before the regal lilies' crown
The ruby-throated humming-bird's green wings
Made a shadow on my white page.

When breathing breaks in the breast
The waves of the ocean,
Listeners for the next wave,
In silence,
Know the tide which has turned at midnight
Will be fallen by morning.
Like swallows that circle and follow the mower,
Before You came, O Christ,
Time like a swan caught up with me
And beat me between his wings.

O Saviour.
You enfolded the dying.
Until we hear that loud,
That difficult breathing stop, and stand alone,
When you demand the impossible
Opening the door You stand in Yourself,
So we surrender the dying.

O birth in death. The darkest rose fades blue,
Even the ocean dawn spreading opens.
Greening
The gold wave foams lily.

On wind-wrought corners of the world
Sand beach or shingle flowers the sea.
Swift blossom azure petals.
Slow moves rain swept grey rose.

Wind frozen wave petals
Of the winter ice rose,
Sea fire sparkles water,
Thorn flames of sunlight.

Petals cool with dew, the hand that dies,
In coma wasted to bone has lain, yet brushes
The cheek from habit once more, suddenly;

When falling a rose or snow as wanly hushes,
There is silence to express the parting for always,
Master of the silent close.

The blue rose of evening darkens rose of night,
And stars that fall in silence like seeds of light.

Rise, morning star in the rose of dawn;
Sun in the blue rose of day.

Icicle Butterfly Tree

The leafless tree
Stands, rooted:
Spirals a gold apple dance.
In the winter oak
Wind sounds an ocean.
Looking in the sun I see
An evergreen snow mantles
Icicles trim,
Silent calm withdrawn
As though there were no wind or all beyond.

Evergreen the winter night enhances,
Crystals with candles the sun flames,
Points prisms;
Airy chandelier the wind rings tinkling,
An icicle tips each branch snow ladening
Curves the wave crest
Under angel's wing sweep.

An icicle star changing colour stays gold.
Heart skips a beat of the rainbow,
Then twinkles a poising butterfly;
Glistens the buttercup of crystals strewn
On golden mirrors; yellow petals
That flight of butterflies resettles.
Eurydice's in the meadow.
The parting night's star kiss within her eyes
Soon paling shows the sun will rise
Before the moon has set,
And open buttercups that crown her hair,
Fall butterflies who wander through this air,
And poising on curled blue forget-me-nots,
That muffling fill the full May springs,
Fan their wings, or close their shadows in them,
Or spread them to droop slightly forward down,
Or eyelid shadows drift on air above the buttercup.

While mist veils a gold field of wheat
At the border of morning swallow hill is blue
With chicory a flock of goldfinch stars eat,
In the valley meadow that murmurs with bees
And a winding creek the swallows sweep
A rattlesnake bites the foot of Eurydice.

On a tall pink butterfly bush, hanging with dew
A constellation of yellow swallow-tails
Stays open like pages of a poem,
Then floats on the perfumed air.

The coffin's enormous silence holds you
In time undone by death,
And the face of the empty clock flies
Swallow-tail nights and days,
White minutes and yellow hours
That will carry you away.

Where in green twilights of full moons
A creek winds gold through valley meadows,
And before a dam below the lawn seems as still as Lethe,
The evening star shines on it,
The Divine Light on your life that is passing.

From the gold wave below the dam
I return the moon to its black mirror,
And wheel it smoothly upstream.
The mist rises in the meadow.

One morning a yellow butterfly
Flashes the laughter of a star up your path,
Your spirit asking me to go for a walk,
In the way I wish you would ask me to go,
A butterfly happiness,
Joy that leads me with love,
Hermes; a note from the lyre of Orpheus,
A grace note of Christ.

While a man circling earth in space is the first
To see the sun rise several times in one day,
The yellow swallow-tail butterfly whose wings
Are marked with black that chases the swallow-tail night
Whose black wings end in blue horizons,
Inside the mulberry tree's green fountain
Between leaf curtains that reach the lawn
Of the marigold garden, I watch the butterflies
Whose swallow-tails broke in the dry summers of the war,
And the day of the atom bomb in the katydid heat.
My company in many tragedies, migrate in clouds.
Next year the garden will be gone. I go
To follow the Indians to the woods in woe.

The moon with a golden torque
Like a dog-tooth violet's petals
Passes through ancient night.

I would have held You
Only the way the bloodroot's leaves
Surround without touching
The tall stem of the flower,
A chalice white and faintly pink,
Frail as April birds' eggs,
When still the woodlands
Rustle with dead leaves,
Turned and returned,
Wandering and huddled
Refugees over the earth.

Early on Easter
The wild geese fly victory Vs.
Where the last snowdrift lay
At the edge of the woods
Still leafless like grief,
Snow flakes
Bloodroot clocks
Of light waves float swans
Whose golden eyes' white eggs
Open stars that hold
The phoenix green egg in gold fires.
Holy wan gold wild lily
The west wind turns the wood green.

The lost
Through wood-doves call;
Though frost
Bend down the daffodils' gold crown
To grass
The sun will lift them up to live in a gold cloud.

Sun frill
Daffodil,
Yellow as meadowlarks that sing on the hill
Like violins' sweet happy voices.
Wind spill
Violets on valleys and fields till spring rejoices.

At the foot of the rainbow's yellow arc
The sunlight's golden cloud
Lights the daffodils' star cups
For the meadowlark.

The icicle flames the daffodil
When Orpheus on the hill of purple violets
Calls Eurydice through April woods,
Follows a yellow swallow-tail butterfly
Where snowflakes become the white stars of bloodroots
And mayflower buds their green parasols shade,
To Springdell where Echo calls her;
He plays his lyre for Pluto
At the tulip poplar's foot
Where the long yellow bells of dog-tooth violets
Open to lift stars and crowns.

One subtle beautiful dell faery angel,
Hermes in a bronze helmet lifts a petal
That flames above his face while the others
Rise a yellow star bell of petals
That recurve a crown.

The rain sprinkles
The dog-tooth violet king's star crown
Of yellow recurving petals
So each tip twinkles
A star.

Flame the promise of the grain of corn,
Run star, cradle the forest,
Flying gold crown
Holy Spirit with a lightning face
Lead us to the vision of God
To see the spirit of man perfected in Christ,
We must become to express.
Fly me a welcome in woods.

Dog-tooth violets run
Like star children in the sun
That lights the creek
The way Christ shines on Orpheus, the Greek.

You of whose existence we know only indirectly,
Welcome us that we, greeted occasional angels
Who step behind you they gloriole,
Acknowledge our union for self-destruction,
The marriage of man with his shadow,
For the separation of the self from the world of creatures,
The loosening of hands that clasp in creation,
The marriage of man with his death.
In sunlight we are joined on the earth
By the weightless feet of the shadow.

When Orpheus turns around
To see if Eurydice is following him,
His shadow falls upon her, the earth's on the moon,
Till Hermes' shell fire aureoles her
With a silver rim before her total eclipse,
Amber like dates on the mahogany dark
Too suavely brushing a dew pearl from her brow
For one who turning in that valley feels
The river's mist rise coldly in her face;
Orpheus, raising his hand in longing,
Feels the farewell gesture poising,
Reach of welcome to darkness,
Sees the flame of his pileus
Candle in Hermes' halo, reflection.

In the wood the dog-tooth violet's yellow star
Lowers a long gold beam while the sun departs.

He who in contemplation seeks the truth
In the Holy Spirit's light can lead the shade
Of his divine creative self to life,
And Trinity live born in death
When God fulfills His promise;
Love turned back on the Creator
Recreates Him, Individual,
His own creation,
His will most free in choosing truth from symbols,
When God commands him, born the guardian
Of one mysterious deep woodland spring
To form it Fountain, poet, lift a shell,
The water's sounding lyre wind modulates.

When dew glitters for joy on the most delicate fern
Star feather, crystals the points of strawberry leaves
That lift green hearts a breathing silvers,
Holy Grail of golden sheen where He lays
The crystal winter's egg; He preens His spiral wing
Till it uncurls the single eye at its tip, and flies.
To warm the heart
Green flames fly up the ferns stems of green stars.

  Like water that falling curls in wreaths, fern
      Angels burn
   Fountains that exhale coolness, perfume
      Stars flame,
  In which the phoenix springs green plume.

By the clear spring, curled in a veil of dreams,
Embryo of creation and the beatific vision,
The fern child unwinds a star of wings
Around the single eye of vision they shield
And will unfold in flames.
The green star's child
Holding an eye in each hand,
Bringing visions from birth to feel joy
To the winged heels of their green curled feet
That point toes to fly real;
The green winged visions on the stem plume.

Green wings, a fern star angel bows to the sun,
Adores in prayer, inspires prayer.
Above the green sheep's wool of his face
A flame on his head flows backwards
With his green wings that he crosses.

A fern unfolding a flight of wings, ladder,
On the top flight the fern child runs
With a commonwealth of arms and legs to the sun.

I heard the April bees
That climbed with sunset up the apple trees,
Like mountains blossoming white petal snow
To bud egg's peaks in visions pink after glow.
Bees work although November's lion yawns,
Build honey domes, await the Blue Rose dawns.

Entrance me tree of stars and butterflies,
Stars of snow crystals and flowers.
Entrance me icicle,
Whiten diamond calm waterdrop,
Hang resplendent pendant of clear glass;
Or weeping pens write in the snows and sands;
This tree this pen this icicle my all
Will vanish snow smoke.

Icicle's eye: see my trees in me.
I am crucified because I love
The Lord of the Fruit Wind,
And thrush-breasted dawn:
Tree that perfumes the wind
And blossoms full white for a golden bird
When the wave at the ship's side throws a rainbow
And foams wide for the shadow of mast, nest and crosstrees.

Tree the shape of a lyre, overflow with flowers,
Sparkling, perfumed, murmuring with bees,
The song of David, and Orpheus, my song,
Of youth, hope, love,
That on the winds of evening
Flows petal notes of unseen terrible martyrdoms.

Green wand
Tree of green stars, rose crowns in a sapphire sky,
In whose branches I ride the wind,
Welcome me the phoenix
In a sapphire palace of roses.

Welcome me birth in death,
My icicle fells the tree
A nest that sails to evening
Star within the rose.

Iceberg afire on night's self-questioning seas
Where clouds dart red lightning, listening seek
The symbols silence frees like falling stars
In song that shines a drifting crystal peak.
Rise from the stem of sleep a burning star
To flash with fire in the snow brain's ice rose.
Seek truth intensely since between extremes
Of ignorance of ourselves and God is born
Our life our tragedy, light's darkening close.

Burn till the singer and the song are one.
Consume darkness to saffire; light
In consciousness the child who says the sun
Follows him where he walks, forgets at night,
The morning star that points, wait for the sun.
Time is different in love as though told by a swan
From whose beak drops falling in calm make
Stars, circles and all the universes.
Silence sings when through skull's echoing caves
Far swan songs on magnolia afternoons
Join vision and the voice within the head,
The lily's gold-tongued phoenix lightning laves.

Our eyes may never hold the sun at noon
Or from ourselves the ice rose waters lift
Measure how darkness spreads until we prune
The rose above its thorns, a pyre, and drift
The phoenix nest; until the rose foams black,
Petals unwind like waves around a rock,
Grow tidal roses from eternal seed.
I sing myselves to death yet singing moves
Night back a little round a pyre that glows
Where darkling the icefire phoenix whirlpools rose.

Crow chanticleer.
Blow out the chandelier.

On the first hot day
A snake frightens Orpheus away.

Farewell, farewell,
Springdell.

At the eastern gates
The night shepherd waits
With his crook of stars,
A question mark above the east.
O past that lights the future,
Where are you now? When
All that splendid company is gone
Except the morning star, rise sun.

The Egg

All the bells
Ring your name.
All the bells
Every hour
Startle your name
From my heart.
Birds from rest
Startle; rise
Sweep and resettle,
Wings poised,
Refolding, still;
Name and bird.

Wind-rounded rose buds twined in grapevines
Hide the robin's blue eggs, secret nesting place,
Till curving petal's rose crystal egg shines
And grapes of rain star the wine-dark rose.
Look how He droopeth down His head.
Rain crystals fall from it.
Christ; Rose that darkens on the tree;
By blood that petals starring lily's rise
Show us the way from martyrdom to Thee;
Save those whom war and hatred crucifies.

Till birds sing in the lion's mouth bright horn
Peace lily call through blown red rose's pall.
Green star snow miracle turn me a fern
In the green valley wood's cathedral hull.

We nest like swallows in the lion's maw.
A black sky thunders where white lilies blow.
Between the egg and death's fast-falling jaw
Save us kind archer Son with love's rainbow;
Feather birds arrows in our cracking shell,
Drawing us back into blue rose green vein
Shoot us wing swift up in the lightning's bell;
Seed faith to rise and risen faith sustain.

What archer stringing sunbeams tries the rainbow?
What arm bends, strains all colors till they glow
A bright arc?
What arrow
Poises once, and to what far point flies
Through egg-shell skies
The lark?

Rainbow-hung bell thunders parting fear.
Although when lightning struck the lily tolled,
Can you rewind the rose to bud one year
Or bird's sky-sweeping wings in egg refold?
O green snow stars descending;
One lily petal's overlapping shades
Snow crystal shadow while the rainbow fades.

When caught in green ice grotto night's crevasse
I saw the star snown Michael brush the brows
Of mountains; wings spill the blue rose and pass
The morning on. Christ radiant in the lily's
Tent of noon help me to wake and praise
The rising star that climbs above the alp
Before the crown of stars and sparking rays
The archangel Michael's sword that slays
The dragon communism. O light green flakes
Your storm hails miracle of snow star-cakes.

On fruit winds swung the lily echoes back
The voices that survive the rose's foam.

Plume me the golden tulip poplar tree
A gloria.

The Black Lily

We are the martyrs, victims
Whom the vicious tried to kill in private;
Released we returned to life,
Explorers of the land between life and death,
The no-man's land
Living death.

Who welcomes the dead
When they return,
Come home?

Living death's dark land
Where no white lilies grow,
Gardens of evil
And green snow,
The waves on windless strand.

The resurgent dead are shadows,
Burn alone.

Eyes worn by windless spaces,
Eyes accustomed to darkness,
Our eyes are avoided like strangers.
The living reject as lost
Messengers of unwelcome wisdom.
Man learns to preserve the unknown,
One black lily enhancing white lilies.

Man's love, our daily bread,
We see fear turn to stone.
In living death of martyrdom
Senses and nerves are strung
By regret, humility;
Death vibrates, wrung
In winds of sin,
The song of black lily.

For us there was hardly spring and little that resembled love
Before the jealous drove down blackening all.
The wind turned the petals of the rose black
From which on invisible stems of heat flames shone.
Turning the black petals to uncover blue ones
That burn,
I saw the wind blow the black petals,
Undo the rose. It was gone.

Why do we dread our form's distortion
In the eyes of others,
Or sweet love's change,
Knowing ourselves and our reflection
A skull of flowers
That unknown Hands arrange?

Break heart or learn
Blood floods the brain,
True love asks no return.

When light dies from the eyes of love
We shall not meet again.
We walk blind in the mind's grave
Who will not see again.

The poppy flames conceal
A black star burnt on petals
Where pollen trembles,
And so our eyes reveal
Death's shadow-shuttles
No smile dissembles.

Rain blood, hail bones, O shattered host,
Pour down in bones and skull.
To raise from death one Lazarus, Christ
How many do you kill?

In the ferocious heat of July, frustration and injustice,
"The angel of the church in Philadelphia"* lilies says
This city of fratricidal hate is a center
Of the organized crime of psychiatry,
The "perverted science"† of sadism.
Rise martyrs,
A sunpath of Philadelphia lilies,
A throng of glory: marvelous stars,
Lift yellow chalices for sunlight,
And orange amber petals that curl flames,
Like fire that survives a flood of injustice.

* Revelation 3:7.
† W. Churchill, "perverted science."

Frost in moonlight grows the white fern
On my window glass
In cold intense as fear,
The white pear tree in moonlight,
The absence of colour on the fields at night.
What monster clambers from the midnight well?
Bound on the rock by rage and despair at injustice,
Indistinguishable from the ugly angel,
We see the abyss at our feet,
The valley of the black lily
Where the shadow appears
At the place of the skull.

By the dark river in the paling sky
The black tree of black fruit turns green with gold stars,
At the cliff's edge, drop to darkness;
Sunlight continues the land, bridge for angels,
Seen when the world's end opens.
God strikes with lightning the way we serve Him
Yet stand in the wound that draws lightning
Since there darkness opens.
From your hand He takes your talent so swiftly
You hardly believe you gave all,
Yet see between your fingers unburning flames,
And in your heart a stump on which to set
Another tree, a flowering skull.
An ecstasy of hatred lights compassion's face.

Red tree the sun illumines
Crimson against blue sky, in autumn,
The first to turn, tree of ecstasy,
American Indian martyr, Jesus tree,
What paradox in the rose's form and sweetness
Deceived us to resolve love with sacrifice,
Turning man's will to God against himself,
The dark declension of man's will to God;
The imperial wood's green word a leafy evil?
Over the crimson wild cherry apricot leaves
Plume gold. The god's mouth opens for sacrifice.
Once more descending O man to death and shadows
Compromise not with evil to rescue love.
When you return to life with knowledge of evil,
Tell the truth about your murderers.
When sorrows age, white wine of autumn woods,
You will still warm yourselves by colors of trees.

Though hate torture lies can twist all
Virtue truth to kill the soul,
Still love's water light may crystal
Triple lily's silver petals, curl
Them moon-horned shell
Of stars, one glistening pearl
That glows with green and rose
Stars the Spirit blows
Till the gold star's fountain flows
Phoenix listening in his dream
To beg vision death to send him home,
Let dew warm in darkling rose,
Ripen dawn seed golden gloam,
Lily fed the sense repose.

Cross that stars the green grape,
Green stars falling where the vine flowers,
Shining, rose sepals enclosing petals;
Enfold me, Christ of the fruit wind
That breathing lifts the roses,
Louder blows the wide leaves of the grapes,
In the green star,
The wind rose.

We nourish the seed You cherish.
You love us as we ought to be,
Ignore all but the secret seed,
The star core.

Rose, star of evening,
When your golden pollen seeds in falling,
Lights the black lily;
Darkling
The original and thornless rose fades blue,
The fruit wind sings of birth in death, the star,
Windrose that flowers in silence
When day springs lily,
Whitens sun at noon.

Snow crystals grow in clouds,
Six-pointed like the lily,
Prayer of the morning star,
That rays like early mists held in the strong
Son's hand to fade against his wrist's
Gold brightening hair.

Lord of Eternal Love,
Give me strength, courage, purpose,
To work all the days of my life;
Make me worthy of love
Worthy a son a Christ
To keep the world from war.

If Green Flake White Lily snowed
Once, crystallized
Love in the lode-
Star; moons of black flakes fall a trifle,
Can realized
Sin ever stifle
Snowman's voice in shuffling veil,
Or flashing
Star flake melt to fade and pale,
That splashing
Blues and ices rose-fire hand
Lifted up in no man's land?

Who enters darkness, solitude, despair?
What star of roses breathing in my skull
Makes lilies burn unburning, flame the air,
That angel stars swim gold in Michael's hair
Whose flowing golden river's snow waves lull
Them blazing on archangel arm and shoulder?

In the dark garden
Star alights on Lily,
Star lily, silent bell:
Star fruit in flower light.

Who comes toward me
Through the silence, snow and darkness,
Light that burning sings of love?

Faith;
The angel of birth in death advances.
O welcome angel. Life is living death.

Back still unborn, nor touch me. Look, my candle
Streams up between us. Stand a little off.

Why does your candle sing, rainbow the sun
A child squints peacock feather through his lashes;
Blue eye in green gold wing,
Blue rose in candle flame's white fire wing?

Accept the song of birth in death,
While Spirit kindles soul
In rose of ashes phoenix egg,
The candle lights black lily urn,
A star of gold
Snow crystal bell to lead you from living death.

How can I hold a star and also hear
The phoenix sing?
His egg stirs in my lily's rose of ashes,
Pearl whose orient lights the lily.
Who are you angel?

Star, cross in darkness unseen,
Gold white and green,
The shadow lily, phoenix urn.
Wanly at dawn
Light will burn
In the valley. Cold as morning, drawn
To know what we believe is true,
Lest our dead stars falling through
Your light seem burning, let us circle
In your orbit, sparkle
As the rose turns blue.
Sun star: darkle
Whom you will renew.

Darling, lift your dark eyes' lashes.
Lily snows what lover gleans.
Fountaining star sparking splashes
Flaming egg with flake that greens
Phoenix in the rose of ashes.
Singing thunders song. He preens
The lightning's feathers, golden flashes.

Snake, why swallow bird's egg, mourn
Flesh devouring soul's relief?
Bound the dull grey stalks of corn,
Burn white stars, fire lily's sheaf,
Smelt the phoenix who is born
Gold from winter egg of grief
To sing earth's shell's a green veil torn.

Away, black snake. Never twine or hiss
In virgin woodbine, clematis.

Spirit of the gold-winged sandal,
Phoenix sprung from egg to candle,
Love that lives in song.
Christian, guard the truth you handle.
The way is lonely where the winds are strong.

Tell me the way to knock.
Where is Christ, the door?

The song that simplifies your feelings leads
Where angels cluster a blue rose of wings
To warm the golden seed, the light of men.
Follow the candle questioning its symbols.
Follow your longing to be loved
Until it becomes your way to approach the truth;
The problem of love becomes that of truth,
Your relation to death.

When the phoenix turns his emerald head
And crest of three feathers,
Along the throat of night
A lightning line of emerald shines
Next to the red gold orange on his neck
That defines his head and firelight
In a molten moment turning yellow green
Gold to his shoulders
Meets the sapphire wings of day
And breast of night.

Rose Lily Chalice of Eternal Light,
The flowering fountain, lift the host of stars;
White Star whose center holds a star of gold
That flames the Word, all the world is vain
Except for Me, I alone give love; forgive, enfold
All men in mercy when You raise the slain.
The sun still sets through prison window bars.
Love, whiten our black lilies. Snow green stars.

Above the ocean's sunpath on snow cliffs
Gold flames rise through crystal stars, the lily,
White leopard,
Whose spots of rain glow in their shadows the sun illumines,
Eyes in the silken wings the gold-shouldered angel,
Swan lily,
Mantles to glisten for the Queen.

Who are you angel?
Snow flakes poising clothe you with stars.
Emerald light flames on your wings' snow crystals.
A dove sweeps in the straight lily's curving petals.

You must still find the rose that welling light
Consumes your candle star
To burn a shadow for the Son of morning,
Like the swan on the sunpath bathing in crystal
That scatters gold stars on his neck that arches the rose spray.
May God now fruit your vision while His Son
Will green heart leaves till stems hide tightly curled
Blue grapes which clustering black are nightly pearled.

Brush, push aside
Leaves. Lush hearts hide
The firm and purple coolness of the grapes.
Now pluck the bunch of poems autumn shapes.

Fill up the skull,
Bone cup, lip full
Of song wine whose bouquet
Will not be lost
Though all else may decay.
My head, death tost,
Float singing in the flood
Waves of blue stars the gentian host:
Contrast the mountain rood.
The fountain star plume sparkles Christ.

No. I am not like the fountain
Though we rise anew from ourselves,
Unless the wind bends us aside
And blows the rose of our fall.
Look. The leaf undone by the wind
Falls only once through the fountain.

Bouquet of plumes: and lilies:
I look for your joy of diamonds and water;
And hear when a cloud is parting
The fountain containing the rainbow
Speak of the sun,
Grow voice of acceptance.

O child seeking the rainbow in the fountain
Through which I see you
While I burn a candle in a crystal lily
Though the afternoon is calm and windless blue;
The sky an ocean over us;
Look at the golden circle round the sun.
A purple cloud glooming the horizon's wooded hill
Cuts the blue sun rose of the golden circle
To arch above the fountain's flowering lily
Corona rainbow rounding a black egg
In which the sun burns white and whitening gold
Phoenix descends into the fountain lily.
The egg becomes an orient pearl.
He who sees the vision knows the meaning
When he who questions also answers look.

Feel the tension in me as morning. Ask dawn,
The virgin of dissatisfaction, why must she,
Always the mother, give the fruit of our night to the day,
The child our grapes
Where darkness enfolds our waters so fruitful
You weep between her lids who most woman
Alone can possess in one moment both child and lover?

Glimmering the angel fades and softly darkness
Closes around us, except for the candle he gave us,
That we look in steadily as the lion eyes us,
Then start for the long-sought door;
Turning lift our candle to light the wood.
A skull flowers in silence.
In the beech tree an arched door opens
To the Abbey's choir and high altar.

I have come, Oh Child and Saviour,
Martyred through the cross, Your door.
Angels droop their wings to mingle
Rose that covers You from cold.
Take my lily's singing candle
Light that Your snow-walking angel
Said would find the rose foretold.

Star cucumber gently sow
Seed from every pod;
Cover Him in green star snow,
Sleeping, golden rod
Whom proud guardian angels show
In the night to God.

The Rainbow Shell

When I come to Singing Beach
Blow from inland, wind;
Keep the waves small and few,
Blow the foambows seaward.

If the ocean that I face
Seems too full for waves that gleam,
Death-fire leap, and rustling fade
In the wet sand's glistening mirror,

Let the poor sandpipers run
Up the sand before the waves,
Turn instinctively with them,
Backward to the sea, and run.

Where several gulls descending lift of wings
Will close the ocean's sapphire a white rose,
Wave take wing;
High on Singing Beach children troop and after
One another run to you: fly
Combing the rose that foams round their sandals
In winsome ripples
Recedes
From arrowmarks like sandpipers'.

    Running with the wind from inland
      Sandals press the wet sand silver,
      Running down the cockle stairs,
    Wave wash spirals rose whorl petals.

Wave breaking leaf reverse the scallop's valve,
That fuming surf on sand,
Withdraws through bubbles,
Shelving a wash that shines green
Curls iridescent foam,
Whispers a wistful farewell:
Reverse the petals' fading curve that squares
A bowman's hand-space
Across the arc of the rose:
Or spiral the rainbow whorl,
Petal wave,
Transpose the shell, rose sepulchre.

What hand in one turning uncircles
The star-pointed spirals of shells
As they wind moon-wan to the stable
That shadows a shining rose?

What hand in farewell rising
Can reach into welcome farther
Than waves extend pale water
Before advancing wine?

Shelve ochre Singing Beach empty
From windlestraw peachblow dunes
To ripple mark driftwood dun,
The sepulchre Mary turns from
And holds her hand as Christ
In pointing the sun rose shell
At dawn completes the spiral
The welcome of farewell.

Pour steady wind from inland
The love of creaturehood,
That all who turning backwards,
Or faint at dead-lift fall,
The Christ Beachcomber raises;
No broken wave is lost.

Love's not the last wave's shell.
Its radiance of the deep,
Its shining colour spell,
Vanish in hands which keep
Which seek, what sea voices tell.

Singing Beach

The seagull's feet print the sand with bows and arrows
And anchors that start wander and vanish
Like the Holy Spirit.
I walk inside the wave's reach so looking back
No mark is left by me arrived a bird where I am.
Wash and restore my soul.
Prevent me until withdrawn in sunblueness; love,
I feel all that I am alone;
Over a small wave's silvering liquidness
Deepens a rising profounder wave:
Learn the wave lengths, their light their multiple voice,
Hear truly the relapse to silence and a breath,
Oh at the gentle wave rejoice.

Calm sea-waves slide from the sunpath,
Light that flows liquid black on the sand,
Excepting always the wave lip's reflection,
The light of bubbles a shadow divides,
Heard in the mantling wave's overturning
A voice of darkness
While light slides down;
The hollow is shadow under the brightness.
I hear the last wave,
Scarcely a breathing of bubbles receding
And then the next wave sounds more determined;
The voice of a beggar I met.

Low tide, black sea,
At the foot of the sunpath with closed eyes
Listening to the various voices of waves,
Gradual of their stairs of light,
A presence turns me around to look.
Only my shadow
Is visible to me on the sand.
The sun is warm
But I who step back when the waves approach
Withdrew before the beggar's toothless mouth,
A throat or lungs diseased.
Still there is no one here but God and me,
The alternate waves upon another beach.

I walked behind the inland wind to sea;
The Beachcomber after me, walked
Before the Inland Wind. I followed Them.

Where the beach slopes so gradually
The occasional waves break far out:
A night, combing black hair with a silver comb
Slow waves flash light.
How long it takes for one slow wave to gleam
All down a beach.

From the east the mist on the grey ocean
The seeds of the sun, grains of corn,
Float stars, dog-tooth violets in the dark woods,
Rise in the green wave's advancing mountain
That catches stars, light and fire
Illumining minerals
So the glass mountain flames with jewels,
Stars,
Still moving forward grows till on the crest
The snows appear
And the wave mountain bending foams to doomsday;
Liquefied the world disappears in a cobalt bomb.

Death on the horizon over the ocean;
The peacock sun spreads its dark tail,
A corona of majesty;
And reflecting on the sunpath silvers each wave
The neck of a sea-peacock that lifts its tail
White and silver feathers to greet those
Of the horses in the moon queen's slow procession
That flows the Virgin's train of lilies,
And promise, victory, the miracle
Of each wave's oracle
That sun looking out of the wet sand
The eye in a peacock's feather
Follows me along the beach,
And stands the sun's corona,
Shield above the sunpath
And the crests of shining helmets
Where the waves of heroes pour
Lives and love for Christ and freedom.

The ocean begins when I come, darkness and light,
Passion tide, the slow walking on of waves.
Astound me wave silence, proceeding silver,
Tremendous and manifold your sliding in;
Wave sight into sound;
Profound expectation in turnover,
Profundity loud moving forward.

Unroll your royal blue field, ocean,
And fire opal, swell green precipices snow cliffs
Foam leaping down ruffling forward
On the pellucid sands,
Slide moon lilies whose stars fade seaward,
And swell rising waves
To break on them and doubling still the third
Break farther out,
This pouring on dare greatly and take
Mind or be lost
Like knowledge given by dreams and agonies
That show our lives in one another's,
Waves in the ocean of God,
And all a Spirit: gull
Returning to the rest
In the morning ocean's lull till the wave rising
Mountain lifts them to fly over the crest,
And comes fullness of roses
Smoothly in silence moves on.

When the green ocean's lilies break in bloom
Brilliant and beautiful
The children I might have had
Come flying down the stair waves of existence
To the gold world of gladness.

Not till the greenness is gone
Waves break white sound,
Boom and a tumult advance
People or thoughts in revolt,
Widening seem nearest when already
Glimmering through bubbles they pass to the ocean
And mark the sand with roses.

I was the cozy lion once
But now I am terrible memories.
Since those I loved sacrificed me
I can do nothing in the sun and strangly green
Cluster the seaweed grapes, a delicious sliding of foam.
How near are the dead?

The superb white Paradise mantles his tail.
In the combing wave the shadow of his plume
Listening to the tragical doom:
"They have murdered me,"
It would be nice to die
Were death as smooth as the glistening sliding
Of the receding wave's sigh and kiss
When the foam's crystal dome vanishes.
Frail are man's freedom and civil liberties.
Come where the rising wave's exceeding light
And forget the hiss of evil.

When sunlight beads the sleeves of foam
That cling along the hero's arms,
Rose shadows under waves move on
Snow meadows to the violet sands,
Through the mountain wall light silvers,
Green ascending wave to snow cliffs,
Raphael look for me a moment,
Green face lightning's shadow dims.
Kiss, O light, the nape of wave neck
Where she throws her long hair forward.
Flame, O light, the brow of anguish,
Darkening till the snow crest foams,
Avalanche crumbles entirely,
Nereid vernal wave swims down
With sunlight for the sea's blue urns.

Under the Christmas Eve snow curved
Like the combing wave and the wings of swans,
Their icicle necks depend in the door of the ocean cave.
Their crystal beaks drop tears and lay eggs.
Percival watched the swan's icicle clock
While he looked in the sea-horizon's blue eye
And in St. Michael's armory broke off
An icicle sword, holding its point up
To the sun, aghast felt Grace withdraw,
Knelt down and prayed to find the Grail that year.

The sun shines through a crystal hand,
While from its lengthening finger
That points down, water runs,
Oracles when roofs and graves fall in.

Icicles the clairvoyant weep their complicated deaths
While they destroy themselves and want to live;
Deaths we are implicated in
Because we did all that we could to save
The victim of the private spiritual murder
Who explodes in tears,
When icicles crash from the cliff;
A tide of stars rises in crystal cove.

O sun I see through waterfalls
That veil me in the rock,
The icicle's eye from whose tip gold doves take flight;
The final constant dropping of your tears;
The Sun path leads from the ocean cave.

A snow hill point in the ocean is seen
Through an east window that reflects
The sun setting over the beach of golden waves;
And makes a vision.
The sun sets in the east;
Descending the snow hill,
From which a gold pool flows in a stream,
Thor-wolf enters the Holy Fell,
Looks out; golden door, vanishes.

By the cradle Saint Michael says to grim Grendel:
"Anger the King of England's angels
And His friends the eagles whom I defend,
And you will find yourself, fiend,
On the edge of my sword which is a prism
To divide the light of the soul into the rainbow
And release the prisoner
When it descends to hell with the brightness
Of Christ to act for the Godhead,
Silver ascension in the wave's shroud and chrism,
Promise He will save him from you
When the evil washing his brain, strive to destroy his soul."

Mounting stars of living waves
Saint Michael in emerald and diamond armor
Flies wind of light;
And seems to stand on wind
Descending gull,
To the still iridescent wave
That dreams the kiss of peace to vanish in light
When in the ship of lilies gothic shadows
The green star's crystal tear
Weeps the ocean full
To be woken by the diving of waves opening lilies,
Breaking green stems to fly swans.

Speak not of despair;
Iris castle of sand at the wave's edge,
We build expecting the tide,
Who children the waves chase, sandpipers,
Turn with the wave aggressor,
Pursue the receding to catch only foam,
Or skip in the wave laugh, wave comfort.
Warm air of roses blown in from the ocean,
It all depends on the day
Whether the wave breaks into rose petals,
More slowly blooming, unfolds the iris.

Purple the ocean when dawn and evening
Lift day's iris castle,
Remote unburning blue,
Over the castle whose sand walls the wave smoothes,
Folding around or running beyond, enters not.
We, ever impatient, channel a path for the ocean,
Children wait not for the tide; build,
Leaving the castle, not even a wave remains in,
Man's citadel, gone.

Ocean: blue roller bird:
Day of luminous blue;
Sun, reflected as myriad lights in the sea's mirror,
Revealing Yourself differently to each individual;
A flight of iris angels castles in Christ,
Three petals enfolding a star dove that feathers dayspring
Whose wave lip rising opens the fountain's mouth,
When gold down the grape wave pours the lion's voice of the ocean.

Wave that combing snow cloud stands mountain,
Citadel from whose peak a cloud withdraws foambows seaward;
Eternal landscapes of clouds
Multiply light and snow mountains
Across the ocean and around the land
A range of angels
While a shell cup moon
Pours diving waves upon a crescent beach,
Harbor of stars.
Walk here where there is shade since you arrived,
My dear, Kingfisher son.
Rejoice in the plenitude of mountains,
Their full ascension and stop,
As formidable as justice, as graceful as mercy.

The Fountain

Once you came walking here between black marble columns,
You the long awaited among the bird songs,
You fountain to falling waters, I fountain where Mercury still
Poising is pointing up to the dome of the pearl.
Yes more than ever arising, my spirit of solitude,
Poignance of selfhood and parting wounds me though I would be yours.
Look at the light uplifting of poetry's finger,
Not warning, just pointing, upflungness of being,
Buoyant upon your laughing, you unaware,
While born from the lily of water its seeds are scattered,
Before the green star unfolds the rose.
Flight is forever winging the heels of Hermes,
Bird-sandalled the song of the fountain.
My master is different; loves and remains.

O hands that warn and point, create and crown;
As at Christmas the mother holds, the child reaches and touches;
As your right hand accepts the sacrifice, Your left opens forgiveness,
Pointing and curving the shell, spiral the curving will,
That we who young as David threw the wayfarer's cloak over our shoulders,
May kneel in awe before the arms You spread
In majesty and judgment,
May feel them closing surround us
And say I am You.

In You the individual is always outside in the garden,
Where secrecy is the danger of sacrifice that makes spring ambiguous,
One who is tired and beautiful
The cathedral of air You build with Your breathing.

Till we who are turned inside out can say it is over,
The sacrifice has been made, the dew glitters for joy,
May we who look in the grave in the pallor of false dawn
Recognize in the tendency to start on a voyage,
The approach of revelation.

I have unfolded the tragic rose to you
So when the two halves of the apple fall apart
The new man steps from the seed's gold fountain,
Breaking the sun's circle
You stand a cross, the way of paradox.

In the garden You were presence
But I am left with absence in the vineyard.
I endure alone the darkening of roses;
The fear of radiation of supernovae,
The red sun, the black hole.
Come lovely spring. Open my eyes, morning look.
Help me refrain from silence that You may speak.
We are one.

When the self we long to become is the sacrifice we may avoid,
Give me an image of my fading substance
Because it was my life.

You asked me what the double rainbow meant
Whose fragments shone as we walked up the hill,
But I was silent in the sun's farewell.

The Rose

Star of dawn; there was no shade on the road
But the shadow of the cross
And thorns that flowered a crown of roses.
Oh morning rose from You I turn my eyes
Yet if I turn from light stand my shadow before me
Oh Light whose sun opens the rose you fade.
Since Your head bowed from the light
Those whom the Dawn pursues cannot die.
Shadow rose open the door of light,
The sun's wheat on the water,
A wind of stars.

I saw the rose of blood grow darker wine
So full of shadows is the flowering Christ
Though rain therein from millions of tears let fall
The eye of day through which darkness looks back
Sunlight at me. I saw a single tear fall.
You cannot weep on the cross,
Yet still the crimson roses are full of crystal tears
That fade with the light in Your eyes like the stars before dawn.
When the dew bird of Paradise spreads his wings sparkling,
The dark center of each rose wells stars;
You give Love to adore, then certainty of Faith;
The stars begin in Your hands.

In twilight the crown of crimson roses becomes black velvet
The rain diamonds in darkness, in moonlight,
Beneath the crown of stars,
In the constellation of Christ,
And the crown of the aurora borealis.

In darkness the stars fall with Your blood from the roses,
Wheat that turns gold in the rose's crown.

Crystal the crimson rose
And sun flame behind its jeweled chalice.
Oh rose thou hast disclosed thy golden face.
Invoke the Holy Who alone can look
On all the universes or on ours,
This rose of dew stars with earth's sun
Deep in an outer petal.

My rose He gave you to me.
From His wound you fall darkling
Like the night garden rose
That lightning turns red in emerald.
Sweetness given in prayer
That stills the anguish of the breaking heart
And fills the starving breast with love,
Breathe in my breathing
Endure in my existence.
The anguish of separation from You is intolerable.

When we exhaust ourselves to love those who hate us,
Feeling our failure crucifies You in them
While they kill us,
Under the shadow and lightning of St. Michael's sword
Save us from the ultimate terror that we betray You,
And therefore You abandon us forever.
Save our faith when in the final sorrow
We know we are dying and no one cares but You;
We see Your rose falling above where we lie
And can no longer open our eyes.

Glorious rose in lightning golden,
Sunlight rain in chalice petals,
Smooth cool curving like their crystals,
Slowly fills and sheds rose fountain,
The golden fire
Of the heart's desire.

Stars dawns and roses are Your Spirit,
The blue rose of sunset, the rose crown of afterglow.
Only Your lilies still perfume the mornings, O Saviour,
And calm the gold wells of Your hands give lilies to me,
In the long flowing of gold hair Your perfumes
Below the crown of lilies, green leaves.

Love wells the goldness of roses
And fountain lilies spring wheat.
The Holy Spirit moves to love all men.
Calm the Eternal wells Creative Love.
O crown of lilies, golden wells of dawn
Pour on mankind the fullness of Your love;
Wash in the long tides of returning mercy
The world of darkness, light the Sunpath to peace.

The Alps

Eastward on the mountain's crest, dawn snow
Curves rose petal swan with a star at his breast.
On the lake's calm a swan's down feather,
Curl of the crescent moon, sails
Pearl reflection on crystal,
Curve a sweeping swallow takes, lets fall,
Turning catches in air three times with delight.
Snatches of song, game in the ode of God's silence,
Poet seek only His fame.

To be woken by the beating of swan's wings on water
Is Saint Michael who leans on the balcony of my joy,
While swallows inhabit your air that winds turning backward,
Trail among the swan's rose castles,
Anguish of Dunkirk or Agincourt,
Agony of Marathon and Calvary.

A swan's wing cloud from the snow mountain darkens the lake
Where the swans turn facing the cold wind
And rise to beat their wings on the water.

Thunder: grape clouds. Flash: lightning
Over the tower. Grow: silence before the rain,
The rose spray's long musical phrase.
Darken rose, open door in the courtyard of God.
Straight rainbows descend iris angels
Whose green feet emerald blue stairs.
Splendid along the water moves the Lord's Spirit.

The snow mountain vanishes in a violet grey cloud
Where a double rainbow, with a purple arc
Between it, appearing three times,
Surrounds a rose of lightning, and then white clouds
That parting reveal snow mountains on blue,
While the swans, shaking rain from their wings, thunder on the lake.

Serene and beribboned with breezes
The lake wears a blue silk dress.

The blue lake smooth as silk
Reflects the swans on snow mountains,
And becomes rose at sunset.

In the valley where the murderer's voice
Is too loud for our ears
We know You as absence Truth.
Feeling our life depends on our choice
To climb where You are Presence
Know we live.

Choices and sacrifices
Reveal and veil the truth in faith
Like the sun and clouds
The beauty of mountain peaks.

Son in Your perfect circle at noon
Stand in blue;
Golden grain in the rose of shadows,
Door in the shield of darkness
The corona encircles,
Unite the mysteries of Your nature.

Son in whose burning the rose turns lily
Suffuse in radiance the soul;
While the rose lifts its pale bowl to the light
Extend to the sun You surrender
With the bread of the snows
The valley of shadows, the cup.

White rose,
From Your burning flames rise on invisible stems
As mountains come out above haze,
Their sailing peaks transparent shadows in sunlight
That reveals valleys and the green village,
Illumines the lacunae and communities of our souls.
Oh may we stand unburning in Your shadow,
Wheat in Your light.

On the green alp in marshmarigolds
Apollo waters his horses white as the Jungfrau.
The sapphire and purple gentians,
And the bird's pale green egg shells with black spots,
Contrast like the people who have been here
With the solemn splendor of the Jungfrau.

From the raving noon I entered a wood,
Turning in the green fern shade,
Saw the snow crest beyond the trees,
Angel and shadow,
Combining the mountains and clouds of my nature,
Joining in silence their several voices;
A summer avalanche
That flows beautiful snow falls in silence,
And thunders so the Divine is heard on each level.

Like water that falling curls in wreathes
The green fern angels burn fountains
That exhale coolness, perfume stars flame,
In which the phoenix springs green plume.

When dew glitters for joy on the most delicate fern
Star feather, crystals the points of strawberry leaves
That lift green hearts a breathing silvers,
Holy Grail of golden sheen where He lays
The crystal winter's egg; He preens His spiral wing
Till it uncurls the single eye at its tip, and flies.
To warm the heart
Green flames fly up the ferns stems of green stars.

By the clear spring, curled in a veil of dreams,
Embryo of creation and the beatific vision,
The fern child unwinds a star of wings
Around the single eye of vision they shield
And will unfold in flames.
The green star's child
Holding an eye in each hand,
Bringing visions from birth to feel joy
To the winged heels of their green curled feet
That point toes to fly real;
The green winged visions on the complete
Stem's green plume,
Unwinds a nebula of winged arms
That whirl around his bowed head,
Plumes uncurling eyes
That look in all directions in God
To remember the future and foresee the past,
Then one a question mark,
One a ram's horn unwinding,
And feathers that wave behind him;
Green curls lie on the armor plates of his shoulder.

Uther Pendragon's Indian of Pennsylvania
Weeps at the fall of his wood,
In the secret spring of October
When violets and blue birds return to comfort despair,
And the rose still stands on its green star.

Green wings, a fern star angel bows to the sun
Adoring in prayer, inspiring prayer.
Above the green sheep's wool of his face
A flame on his head flows backwards
With his green wings that he crosses.

A fern unfolding a flight of wings, ladder,
On the top flight the fern child runs
With a commonwealth of arms and legs to the sun.

Above the snow mountain's rose wings
In a blue sky the full moon
Ascends like a white balloon
And floating over the alps, shines.

Swans entering a black lake,
The snow mountains appear in moon light.

Morning star in a rose sky;
Long rays from dawn's regal lily
Light the snowpeaks rose, then white,
While Your Presence withdraws beyond them,
Altars where we offer Your Sapphire Rose to You,
That the sky unfolds while the sun appears
Star, gold and rayed by the snow mountain;
The valley opens green.

The snow mountains shining praise You.
The stars ascend: gentians, buttercups,
Alpenroses, eglantine, edelweiss.
You stand us in the shadow of the rock on the alp,
To see the morning star till afternoon.

Star of the deepest night,
Hope of the saddest day,
Jesu be in the gentian
Spiritual communion for me.

Give me your love from the remote heavens
That I may forgive my enemies.
Shine it in the deeps of my heart;
Star in the gentian,
Morning Star in the gentian skies.

Still the snow peak of hope
Sails through the sapphire sky,
Flying the wind's snow plume,
Incense an angel swings from the cathedral ship,
While foaming avalanches mingle with clouds,
And flowers ascend a rainbow
Over the snow mountain's prow.

What drove the poet up the mountainside
Who hears a warning in the horrible wind
That whistles over the red orchid alp
Before a hail storm in July?
A vineyard between us whose leaves screen the light gold,
Awareness of truth that felt like deceit;
The shadow that walks in darkness,
The voice that interrupting my own
Speaks differently,
When I would have appeased my betrayer
Spoke words I regretted long
Before I acquired their wisdom,
Or without feeling startled by my own sternness
Used their tone on the mean and dishonest,
Raised it as my own voice against injustice,
Like anger whose echo thunders from mountain to mountain
From the Jungfrau, to the Monk, to the Eiger.

Clouds; do snow mountains remember or dream you
To rise from the valley around them at evening
Like men of justice and fortitude
Who held up the sapphire alone?

More beautiful than the crests
Of snow mountains clouds double
Shone your head in its halo of snow bright hair.

We see the greatness of a good person
Like that very rare sight
Of a man's shadow enlarged five miles
Below on a luminous cloud.

Day is dearest blue in the alps
When swallows fly a violet valley.
Its most beautiful hour is a depth
Of shadows, the silence, the long sailing of swallows,
The silk rush of wings, that swift light,
Sail from the valley to the West,
Disappear in the sun that rays down a snow mountain
From which streams a crystal river.

O Light that falls through clouds upon far snows
And fills the crocus valley's purple cup
With a rose wine of mountains seen in storms,
We walk home while shadows close flowers and valleys,
Our side of the mountain darkens
Except for a silver ridge,
Our foot sounds as strange on the rock
As the bird that crying leads us over the snow.

Although the sun neither rises nor sets
Over these mountains
Each dawn and evening their sky is gold
Like the circle of pollen within a lily's petals.

Withdraw in sapphire, sun, and ray a crown,
A lily of light to shine the snow mountain
Angel whose face is blue with cloud shadows;
Stream a wide ray of rose on the snow wings,
Rise to the white cloud mountains
That float over the valley and grow the towers of God,
Become a rose bird flaming angel,
Within whose wings the sky is most sapphire,
Last rose castle that lightnings all night.

Until he appears
In the twilight dew of the flowering fields,
Who hears a star sharpening his scythe
For the light years?

Peace: snow mountain peaks we longed to reach;
Climbing through cow bells that ring bell flowers flashing dew,
We return to spring in a valley of yellow pansies
Where by a cataract that pours from clouds
A line of sheep climbs up into them
Like people I love who die.
White night; you resemble despair at evil,
And memories of those who tried to murder us.
The knowledge of evil appalls.

From tragedies concealed like snow mountains in clouds
Avalanches descend to ruin our lives,
And reason destroying all purpose and hope
Sees love always end in betrayal,
A war approaching to ruin the world;
Alone to witness destruction
A walking wound circles in whiteness
That crystals the spires of crocuses,
And rains sapphires on gentians that furl petal visions,
Where their death knells will be rung by cows
That go down like waterfalls of bells.
Mountains and tragedies remain.
If the powers of evil whelm against us
Send St. Michael with an army of angels,
Airy stars, lilies to save us.
The clouds open on high around
The snow swan flying the crown
Of the Jungfrau on its wings.

From the valley where clouds appear
Rising mist veils the snow mountains,
Angels almost invisible,
Till climbing the mountain through clouds
Ascending to sunlight, above the rainbow
Projected on clouds beneath,
We are shadows that rainbows aureole.
Each porter in a line
Bent under the wheel of cheese he carries,
A gloriole
Across the peaks of Nepal,
Rises the full moon.

We climb to the solitude of the snow mountain angels
And the Silver Horn with snow hands
That receive the first and last light,
Messengers who help us to find the Truth,
Unseen, more powerful
Than a range of snow mountains in clouds.

On a mountain top a snow Pegasus lifts cloud wings.
Silent morning! Shepherds climb by gentians
To open the fold whence sheep with bells rush
With the cataract to the meadow of yellow pansies.
Along the green alp red orchids shine with dew.
After the July snow storm in brilliant light
Where pink rhododendrons and buttercups reappear
Larks singing fly out as though above the snow mountains,
And dive toward the valley of cowbells that an eagle
Sails over to the Eiger above which after
The climbers fell to death and froze in the storm
A double rainbow with a purple arc between it
Shone to the Jungfrau and the Silver Horn with snow hands.
The cloud Lamb lay along the mountains.
The cloud Lord put His Hand on the Eiger.

Creator or destroyer,
Rainbow in the dawn's rose sapphire,
Lightning in the sapphire rose of evening,
When we can see the beauty of nature,
Sometimes an avalanche wakes us in sunlight
Where bees pull the bluebell flowers,
The terror withdraws from nature
Like clouds from snow mountains that flower in sunlight,
The tragedies of life from our youth
When we can remember hope and love;
But clear of clouds at noon, the snow mountain
Looks like the revealed mystery of God:
That the repeated sacrifice
Of the United States of America
For freedom has crucified it like Christ;
When the American psychiatrists have tortured
The honest intelligent individual
A difficult love and loyalty are required,
Resignation of life, like the gentian
When through clear air a stream of hail
Moved over mountains, poured on it.

Under the sapphire skies
The wild pink roses open.
On the alp the ruby vanilla orchid smells
Sweet in the silence of pale blue bells,
And the lion's bane like the Pleiades.

The crown of the Jungfrau is flown on the snow wings
Of the Holy Spirit, a dove or swan from whose beak
A ray of light, an arrow, a victory V
Streams down the east side of the Silver Horn peak
An ice roof that shines like the stable in Bethlehem
From which snow hands reach out.

When rivers of clouds fill the valleys with dreams,
O sun withdrawn beyond our world
Shine still on the high places;
When we are in the valley of the shadow of death
Reveal the vision of Paradise to us;
Above the snow mountain;
Rainbow in the rose afterglow,
Edelweiss rays of sunrise.

Light that encircles the rim of the world's rosewell,
Help us to climb in spirit where the horizon
Never fades that in the darkest hours,
Unable to walk in the snow,
Bound on the rock,
We may see the gloriole of the Sun
The path of His approach.

At peacock water, in the poplar
Stand your gold wand fire-wind.
The swan drawn oceanwards by an undertow
Turns his head entirely around to look backwards
When autumn crocuses that have returned the spring
Are cut in the shadow of the mountain between dawn and sunrise
When the snow peaks shine like the scythe the reaper sharpens.
He goes before the dew
That changes colour with each wing-beat
As a white butterfly visits the crocuses.
Others cut like Tibet dry in the hay
That perfumes the wind under the sun's corona.

The Wheat

I cannot walk among the ripening wheat,
The stars that falling stream the aureoles
Where phoenix angels burn ascending spires,
Yet longing at the field's edge hear a voice
In wind that circulates the star wheat; angels
Below green lightning turning golden leaves.
What is the sacrifice? I asked the voice.
To see the green starred grapes beside the roses,
Their leaves enlaced by tendrils of the vine;
The center of the rose a field of wheat.

Always the way fades early.
Straight is the way that circles to where the rose is absent,
Its redness implied in the apple,
The wine on the table where there are no flowers,
Though beyond the window evening whitens,
The soft underside of a fish, sprays flower
The pearl color of all sea-water-born twilight creatures,
When forgiveness hides the sacrifice, a garden conceals the agony.

All who listen by windows all night,
All who live where it is always evening,
Martyrs who long to escape from tyrants,
And still believe the justice of your cause will free you,
Escaping found your legs too weak to walk,
Or walking gold light of grain
Serenely as corn silk
Where silence enleaves the silent
Felt the captors jostle the husk,
Thought how Christ still could have fled
When in the garden of olives
He saw the lights approaching, heard the tumult,
And cannot feel your sacrifice is needed,
Tired and left alone the certainty of value
Fades even more, yet remains.
Who does not quail before the final fire?

Thrust freedom's torch down holes where Europe was.
Hear, blinded while the sparks flow up your arm
On the death wind, the groans of dying people.
They would not hear foreboding intuition
That wind approaching under a purple cloud
Roars like a nearing ocean over hills,
Distantly swells a future that hydra-headed
Blackly hoods the sky, darting the tongues
Of lightning that make dogs howl and run home.
Severed our roots of faith in God and man,
Feeble as hay left drying on the hills,
Caught up and whirled by the cold wind that pours
Out of the thundercloud, we too shall wither.
There is a sound of conspiracy in the wheat.

The ocean's full moon
Throws its gold net over the green wave,
Like sunrise on buttercups in the plumy grass,
And on flowering wild strawberry leaves of dew.
The thrush still sings in the valley wood
Though freedom is almost lost
Whose origins in mist
Like songs of larks heard on the ghostly hills
Where ancient foes listen for enemies
Seem the flying stars heavenly choirs
To the knights of wheat in green pavilions
From whose peaks green pennants glistening with raindrops
Flame and stream plumes above helmets on the sunpath.

They dream till fear wakes them in dawns of thrushes
To lift green helmets, listening ears of prayer,
When the riper ears, guardian angels of golden
Awns bend near. The rainbow walks.
Prepare for war who grisly stalks
Green warriors his axe beheads. His green
Pavilion opening a slit Gawain is seen
Armed in pale green wheat scales a fish.

Green light shines through the pavilion's peak and its long
Flowing pennant of the rain star
When Gawain appearing on the morning of battles
Looks out to speak. I begin to see the end.
It is so big up here where the sun is singing.

When your green hair blows gold from the helm
And flames the hero light around Cuchulain's head
Under dark clouds on Larkstoke
Fear is transformed the splendour of energy,
Flow the wind;
Soul like the lark ascend from the field's deep fleece,
Sing into the wind.
Harvest of larks, bowing lay your golden locks
Across your crown to show your neck green knight;
Bend for the thunder stroke, rainbow.

Your intuition of purpose in suffering,
Your defense of your purpose,
Will be seen in the light of the backward look,
Through the reflection of God in the Godhead,
The self-reflection of the Son from the Father
Creating you creature:
Self, the reflection of the Father in the Spirit
That shining beyond the shadow
Leads the soul darkly to the light of wheat.

The pheasant of golden shoulders
And red and green head,
Facing the sunrise that crimsons his breast,
Calls beating his wings on a furrow
And makes a cloud of dust,
Then walks across the ploughed field,
And enters the wheat.

I saw the wheat take light upon the slopes of dawn.
The Lord said Speak with the accent of dawn.
Over a sea of wheat the sunpath shines in the wind.

From their singing tree on the hill
I climb with the sun lighting the rain on the wheat,
The red-winged blackbirds call
This is green. We shall be free.

Wind in the wheat I walk in the fire of falling stars.
In the shadow of noon sun beneath the wheat
Keep me dew in the green wings of the clover.
Be the still tear in which I live to love,
That while you see through me
I may be your eye.

A wind of swallows waves the sea of wheat,
Fabulous, liquid, living wind flying
A field of fish that open gills when thick
With seeds the head droops Christ. Peacock
The million-eyed sea stands aside.
Wind earing wheat spreads golden awns, star hair.
Though man destroys himself, his world, O wheat,
O dying Sons; if no one migrates
To another solar system leaving us
Buried in silence when the snow descends
Upon the darkened star that was our world,
Our best creations may have been
Ideas of faith requiring miracles,
Ideas like snowflakes in the hand, expiring
Stars that light images the Creator
Sees as part of a purpose He creates;
Ideas like fireflies that rise from wheat
In twilight and darkness and lightning.

When you died the wheat was green
That shines now in a triumphant wind
Like the sunpath you are way out on.

Wheat on a hill doth take the wind
The most beautiful way; Golden Eagle.
O brilliant wind. This was a multitude:
The quick and green, our hopes, the lives we loved,
Our very selves,
These heavy-hearted hosts of harvest,
Wan bearded warriors of war's furnace,
Long dry leaves and ragged rustlings,
Doomsmen of the long-haired stars,
That grey as death ascend the hill to sapphire
Before the lightning reaps the lion's mane,
The rainbow swathe to the last sheaf
The still bare field; and stooks of love
Hide us in thunderstorms until we stand
Between the sun descending in a corona
The moon rising within a rainbow.

Swallow Hill

On the Swallow Hill
Field the deer going through tall grass make
The pollen smoke. In still air,
As though censing angels pass,
Here and there a head of grass
Bows to release a small cloud.

On midsummer eve their barefoot brains washed
Small children strain to lift bales from loads
To put the cross in the barn. The evening star
Seems still, the fireflies in the meadow, moonlight on the ocean.

A firefly in the regal lily
Lights its gold star in the green one,
The Lantern's Christ in Glory of Ely Cathedral.

Watching the firefly tree light up on the hill,
A star paying rent for its palace,
A rose and ten wagon loads of hay,
I see beneath swallow hill
The light inside the open door of the barn
That shadow men are stuffing with clover of fireflies.

When Oberon the moon comes up the dark valley
The fireflies glow green
Above his long gold lantern in Doe Run
Where soon Titania will behold her white face in a ruff.

One July afternoon on Swallow Hill
She asked "Where are my sons? Where are my daughters?"
Then two swallow-tail butterfly stars
One yellow, one dark flying around each other,
Dropped at her feet and made a cross with their wings.
The black butterfly night, facing west, held his wings open,
While the yellow day stood between them facing east,
With closed wings bordered with suns.

Night with day on his back climbed the alfalfa,
And suddenly there was a double butterfly, upside down,
A black serpent of domino spots,
With a head to the east and west.

The night swallow-tail looking at Titania from yellow eyes
In a black head that appeared moons approaching,
Rockets at night,
Frightened her until she saw they were spots on his back.
His large black eye faced north.
His feeler curled in his mouth.

Night's wings enclosed the yellow wings of day
That, when they parted, sunlit, twinkled a star
On the clover where the orange butterflies flame.

The night swallow-tail butterfly opened black wings
With a yellow border, starting from inside, of hearts,
Falling stars, comets, on the wing-tips, half-moons;
At the inside edge of a row of blue squares, windows,
Two yellow sunrise gold eyes above swallow tails.

Two children appeared. Each held
A twig from which hung the chrysalis
Like a lantern; one green, on the top of which
A half-circle of tiny gold beads
Will close before the lantern darkens
Like the other through which yellow wings show,
To watch the butterflies come out they hang
The chrysalis lanterns in the milkweed.

Cumulus clouds rise Windsor castles,
Tall towers with domes,
Vision of the City of God in blue skies,
Of our cities in a nuclear cloud, and grow
From Alps to Himalayas
In the white light and rose afterglow
A Divine Farewell of the beauty of nature to man,
That gift to man to recreate himself;
And of Mallory who lies in the snow of Mt. Everest.
His coat in tatters, flutters, flies
Like butterflies that float in Queen Anne's
Lace, flowers like snowflakes
From the cloud mountains.

Swallows fly
Skimming and sweeping
The hill's clover,
Where swallow-tail butterflies flame for hours
But I am weeping
That all we loved is over,
And more than the flowers
Will die
Where I wait for the mowers.

Across a red and white striped field
Of clover and Queen Anne's Lace, the Milky Way,
Silent butterflies speed Perseids,
Floating gold falling stars,
Yet sail like boats we long for in the country,
Come about very quickly,
Explorers of the summer air and breeze,
Glide into the wind. Above, among them
Swallows fly lovely movements.

Orange tiger lilies lift petal crowns.
In sunlight orange butterflies float
Above the clover as though the August heat
Became lively flames, a ballet of fire,
Or fly the time of love, or slowly opening
Flame on a flower like a stained glass window.

While I sit under the shade of the tulip poplar
I planted on the hill, in the sunshine on the grass,
The black butterflies open yellow victory Vs
Of falling stars on the edge of their wings,
Thin as shadows,
Then higher than a ballet dancer springs up and turns
Around, turning fly together skyward.

Dansez, dansez papillon noire
Avec les paillettes d'or sur vos ailes.

The yellow swallow-tail butterflies
Twinkle on their pink bush
That moves like summer breathing,
Exquisite as the ballet,
Enchanting dance, alone, together,
Or with a black butterfly
Around the pink hawthorne tree.

One August noon a star falling
With face aflame and streaming hair
Under the arc of yesterday's rainbow
Flew over the wood into the field
Beyond the men baling
And the hayload the rainbow turned gold.
Warning how war may start
Was it this hot grey stone,
Or Michael, grown up since the war
Who arrived from England to hunt for it?

The new moon in blue sky,
A boat drops Venus and Jupiter.

The black butterfly with shining blue
At the end of his wings opened them like a smile;
A book of the most important hopes
On the goldenrod covered with yellow butterflies.

The monarch butterfly visits the goldenrod,
The silent departure of summer.

v. 2. The conjunction of the crescent moon with Venus and
Jupiter was on August 26, 1968.

The swallow-tail butterfly suns his open wings
On the Queen Anne's lace and butter-and-eggs that swings
On Swallow Hill while I pray
To stop the hurricane far away
And watch a fleet of yellow butterflies sail
My prayers on their frail wings
Here where it is calm with a blue sky
Like in the eye of the hurricane
Surrounded by walls of terrible winds that destroyed
Jamaica; Cancun, Cozumel in Yucatan,
Passed Santa Cruz and Santa Rosa
In Mexico, and vanished in rain, a miracle.

In the Michaelmas daisies on Swallow Hill
I heard screaming and found a meadowlark
On his back; his body yellow as goldenrod.
He was looking up at me and then he died.
I hid him in the garden in the peace roses
From the hawk that flew low to look for him.
Meadowlark: are you the Holy Spirit
Of poetry and prayer, of Vietnam or peace?

In battle, in war the hand of the Lord seized us
And struck like lightning the leaves from our ears.
We are like the Northern Cross of variable
Stars now paling;
Our sacrifice and the freedom we saved for you
Like golden towers of corn.

The west wind's hunting horn blows the green woods yellow,
And on the hill the rows of tall corn chiefs to rags
That wave farewell.
O papery rustling. We are poor;
An army that holds heavy corn babies.
A stalk falls to the ground with a thud.
The wild geese fly past, victory Vs.
The window panes are falling like tears.
Always departures and longings,
O wind blow not the rose till I come.

Clear morning to harvest the corn
Like brave armies of our history that warn
They fought Cornwallis.

Red tree the sun illumines
Crimson against blue sky, in autumn,
The first to turn, tree of ecstasy,
American Indian martyr, Jesus tree,
What paradox in the rose's form and sweetness
Deceived us to resolve love with sacrifice,
And turned against himself man's will to God?
Over the crimson wild cherry apricot leaves
Plume gold. The October wood is glorified.
Once more descending O man to death and shadows
Compromise not with evil to rescue love.
When you return to life with knowledge of evil,
Tell the truth about your murderers.
When sorrows age, white wine of autumn woods,
You will still warm yourselves by colours of trees.

When the mist of October mornings,
Like smoke from Indian fires,
Or tulip poplar torches, burns away,
The swallows still fly on my hill, I look down
On the Indian summer wind turning green trees
A gold phoenix screen with the sound of seas
And the leaves slow flowing gold
Like the last minutes of the pheasants that walk on them,
Stately and doomed when the shooting season opens
As the Indians we cheated out of their land
Killed and drove West and destroyed their freedom.
The Indian Churchill led the West to freedom.
May the wild geese always fly victory Vs.
Gold winds pass along the top of the wood.
The leaves shimmer like water over gold;
Fall butterflies, sparks of torches, corn,
Till with the first snow in a distant faded wood,
A tulip poplar's golden torch lights the year to its grave.

The swamp maple flames like love to remember
Their sacrifice for our freedom, the green maple,
Seen by the fire opal
One that ruffling grey reflames a crimson ember,
Salmon, amber,
In a gold Indian summer wind that warns
Of fires that burn the barns;
How after autumn like Americans
Who break into a house to rob, rape, and kill,
Went through the cornfields like a nightmare
So they looked like the victims of psychiatry,
The winter tornado rushed in the door
Of the barn and tore it down and killed a man.

If only in our old age
Divine Love would colour our mind,
Like autumn foliage,
The pheasant's plumage.

Like my hope of saving the wood, on Swallow Hill
The roses lean from northwest winds that roar
Below through the wood of Trimble's Hollow
Like bulldozers that making a reservoir tore
Out the west end so on All Hallow tall
    Trees blow down in Springdell
Where in April the dog-tooth violet opened his bell
Of long petals that rise star, cross, and crown, curled
The Indian's vision where the creek purled
In sunlight before their treaty with William Penn.

    A flock of red-winged black birds
   Makes a sound of going like their arrival
  In spring with hopes like ours that to remember
   Is like finding the violets of November.

At sunrise in December snow stars
From an exaltation of meadowlarks in corn stubble
One fell a gold star unconscious on my path.
In the warm house he revived except for one wing;
Radiant looked at shining fields of snow,
A green hill's ice helmet, oaks
White with ice, sunlight silver a branch,
And held my finger with his claw before he died.
I took him up on Swallow Hill and turning back
Saw the sun's double corona before a snow storm.
I held him up to see it in his beautiful coat.
Now man destroys the atmosphere of earth,
We face starvation and extinction.

The snow winds blow all night.
On Christmas morning by white rose bushes
Lightning in falling snow that a pheasant's tail brushes
On it, in sunlight carved in diamond stars,
Long feathers flow and flame, the Holy Spirit.

The Wild Swans
in
Pennsylvania

The glory of woods, tulip poplars yellow,
In sunlight gold above the hollow,
And mellow,
In the lake's shining mirror,
Echo with a pair
Of wild swans rarer
Than silence that facing each other outline
In air
A heart
They lift to Divine
Love through which the sunbeams dart.

Pure white mitres shake
Lightning wings that make
Circles they sleep in, wake.
Frightening them, shooting echoes.
The swan cries and grieves
For cygnets and silent snows,
In yellow leaves wind blows
From a golden crown that glows
In the lake until the pen
Swims in the wake of the swan
That flows
Two Vs
Of silver leaves,
Arrows
From their necks' reflected bows.
Few swans or poets live to old age;
The swans' reflections on the wood's gold foliage.

The white rose swan whose breathing petaled
The river ruffling feathers prest
Snow softly, floats, now calmly settled.
Her swan song rises in her breast.

From the organized crime of psychiatry,
From the horrible injustice of the law,
"Good Lord deliver us."

They call the pure and beautiful insane,
To damage our brains,
To make us like dry corn stalks that a combine,
Green knight with flowing gold beard of grains,
Cuts, then husks
And shells the cobs till winter dusks.
The swan busks
In self-defense and dying
Sings: My living flame of love is flying
On the sunpath to the Lord of Eternal Life.

The full moon
When wild swans migrate in freedom shone
In the dark wood's creek like corn in the stone
Silo till eaten by a black cloud bear blown
Before lightning, a thunderstorm. At dawn
The wild swans had flown
Like love with autumn, the deer and fawn,
From the dark woods and lake, green lawn.

The Swans in Winter

On the day of the first snow in the meadow
The white swan
On the sunpath of the Doe Run
Creek makes
Gold stars and shakes
His wings so feathers float softly down
Like star flakes
It snows on the swans and rose bushes.
The swan pushes
His breast against the ice that breaks
With the sound of the heart of the rose
That seems to send up the afterglows
Near the evening star.

Through the snow meadows, the Doe Run
Winding east in S curves,
The sunlight's silver swan,
Seems from the full moon wan
In the west as memory swerves
Like swallows, grieving sweeps,
Waking from dreams
A love of high romance streams
To the shepherd Lord; leaving weeps.

The Swan's Feather

The Swan's white feather
Held up against the sun path
Shines with rainbow colours,
The oil fire of the Holy Spirit
That saves him in winter weather,
The white orchid with the yellow trumpet.

The Crimson Crocus

Swan of dawn in sapphire thundering
Snow wings strew feather pens, the saffrons,
Dipped in the green star's heart to write lonely;
The Word as clear and real as agony's tears,
When in the sepal's spire of Creative Love,
The silence flowers prayer, the grapes of dew
Gleam on the plumes of dawn's swan quills,
The crimson crocus calls.

Where the beech missal falls
Each year, leaves that frost glitters, scrolls,
Pages of vellum from the Book of Kells,
The swan's arrows pierce together valentines,
Letters from the underground through which crocus pens
Rise stars, vikings in beech leaf ships,
Wan souls of the lost, ghosts of rain or sin,
Refugees from Iona and communism,
From PhnomPenh Cambodia and Pennsylvania,
Green pronounces constellation of angels.

Here the Swan
Divine
Inspiration stuck His crocus pen,
That illumines the margin of winter, a plume of twilight petals
Opening a star of wings that adores in azure,
Initials mystery,
Unknowns of existence that melt in the finger,
Clairvoyant ivory candle for a book
Clasped like the love of the dead in the hand of the living;
The brown beech leaf of holes,
The wounded heart of the stag.

As if from our anguish and partings
Arrows had flown
That fell to earth all at once in spring,
Saffrons beautiful with the dews of oblivion,
Passions faces and kisses,
Tears from the lost past,
Crystalled the spires of crocuses
Purple and white like wampum.

Straight from Christ, feather wet in the crimson muse,
Sing the scarlet deeps, the cardinal skies of anguish,
The purple of loud terrible winds,
The most royal oceans and evening mountains,
Swan who sang up the sun, Phoebus Apollo,
Who waters his horses white as the Jungfrau in crocuses,
Beating wings that wake Peneus, Lake Leman's joy,
And snow feathers and crocus wings
Blue Peniel angel, violet of the sun's heart,
Saffron the song of birth in death,
Inspire our suffering with Christ
Where in green hair apostle white stars whirl
Round themselves prayers flow in flowers;
Sea-shell full of their secrets seraphim eggs
Open extending stars to crow gold dawns.
O be careful in prayer.

Dawn pen the wind moves to write in a green star,
Cygnet of Paradise, signature of the Paraclete,
The crocus whose pearl stem horizons flame
Purple orisons of rose grape wings pointing skyward
Shapes the ice that stills it in crystal
From which the purple tip of a petal escapes.
A snow star alights on the crystal stem
That a star flake, remaining in air,
Touching with a point creates crocus star,
Purple heart in the Holy Grail;
Inspires pen to flower and fly in the Holy Spirit.

The following stars stand on their points on flower and stem;
Snow plume that seems to remain in air above the crocus,
Its crystal nimbus of prayer unseen
That bends it to lie on the ground: a vision of death;
Look in the universe eyes of the angel
With blue star wings to explore,
Stamen engine with six wing petals:
While snow on silver trees changes the landscape of day;
The aurora borealis crowns the night.

When the sun melts the stars and opens the crocus egg,
A swan's containing a phoenix egg,
Pen unfold your wings flying the phoenix egg;
Heart take off for Eternal Love;
O risen Christ look from Your crocus icon
That reveals our spiritual selves,
Flown in the swan's petal wings,
Phoenix Who flowers in wine eclipse petals'
Translucent lively chalices,
When lightning flames Your crest
Preen gold flight feathers,
Winging the chalice well
Inspire the crocus pen to flower in time
For the rainbow to illumine its chalice,
Unfolding a flying star in which three gold angels
With pollen candles hold orange fire,
Phoenix light, Heart's fire,
Guide the missile of prayer,
The warheads of ultimate weapons to explore the stars.

Adoring stars in luminous blue, the saffrons,
Open their purple hearts' wings in the swan's,
Beating in time with the Sunlight Heart of the Godhead,
Flying the cygnet Word in chalice wings,
While over them wing-haloed wasps
Fly slowly golden arches shape of fruit,
Carry the swan's plainsong;
Take all the pollen from grape chalices on pearl stems,
Dear fellows appear in the sun that roots in hope
The flying saffron cups of tomorrows,
When the great dipper will dip up the sun
That fills them with light around the turning world,
Lamps above the shadows.

The saffron closing the sun in a phoenix egg
Folds petal wings moonlight pen
To await Christ in the swan host.

The swan moon mantles her wings
White with fear of the crimes she has seen,
Her doom, reflection;
The dawn's moonpath swan.

Dip in green stars my crocus pen.
Snow flakes,
Bend the long wands
Lifting the heads and necks
Of two swans the lake reflects,
That facing each other outline
A heart they lift to Divine
Love: a Valentine
Through which the sapphire
Waters shine like fire.
Arching forsythia throws
Stars, crystals on snows,
Between wings that mantle white rose.

On the west a line of Himalayan spruces
Waves branches with tips like crosses
To bless the lawn of crocuses
Where under the budding sky basket beech
With a root like an eagle's claw I beseech
The Lord to save us from communism, nuclear war
And asteroids as though from Leif Eriksson,
A viking ship like this beech leaf.

The swan's orison flies
In the crocus dawn's purple skies
And white horizon to the orange sunrise
To illumine the page of a missal
Like the pointed copper beech leaf that stands up
An aureole behind the crocus pen
That in sunlight opens a cup,
Shining like a quasar,
The origin of blue stars and galaxies.
It hails star cakes on the crocus chalices.

If doomsday dawns, holding the pearl stem
Of the crocus, feel the wind, violet violence,
Startling the stars in the firmament,
Glimmering the sacrament,
Forgive the envious arrow, private spiritual murder.
Remember Your promise to Noah in the flood's rainbow;
Save mankind Archer Son.
Rainbow archangel sow your emerald wings
Saffron missile chalice to save the free.

The sun's corona shines the crocus promise.
If You announce the last spring of man,
From sin death earth draw up our souls, O Son,
Radiant rains of arrows and bend the rainbow.
Wing saffron sorrow, flying a blue dawn of stars
Phoenix egg to the cobalt God.
Dawn swan, spread saffron wings in the sun.
Flying the passion He will eclipse the night
You die alone for peace, saint in green flames.

Where gentian days arise between the sun and the moon,
And facing snow mountains from cliffs of alpenrose
Chamois look down on the rainbow,
A crystal waterfall begins in sunlight
When I call on the crimson crocus
That flames by the snowdrift of July
Through which buds rise and open in an hour.
The avalanche answers the thunder.

The crimson crocus weeps. On purple petals
The rain drops grapes and crystals,
Passion, compassion in creative love,
Flowing the swan song from the Christ
Onto the crocus pen that opens the Saviour's heart.
Each seraph spreads six wings around the Christ.
Stars the saffrons fly swan of wine-dark noon
To fill the crimson crocus Holy Grail.
The purple arc of martyrdom appears
Between a double rainbow.

The Sun Path

No day so diamonded or wave can walk from light,
Down the sky beach unveiling light,
Trail the foam peacock's tail,
As ghostily you return my joy;
O day I treasure most out of my whole year's all.

Serene sea evening Queen
When the dying sun looks in Your eyes
Extremely calm between the sun and the moon
The ocean becomes more blue
As silence deepens before snow,
The horizon clear as blue eyes,
The straight look of truth,
When You reveal Your knowledge
Beyond the level of words
Of the attempt to destroy us when we were unconscious,
And star appear in blue
Before the earth turns from the sun.

Star whose clouds reflect the sunlight
And conceal You still unknown,
Love in whom our prayers are living
When we can no longer pray,
Give us Your hand of arrows,
Gather us a sheaf of light.

Waiting: Columbus on Jamaica's shore,
I watch the rainbows arch my dead ship's hull,
The conch shell's horned moon sail its pointed star;
Or on a twilight ocean
The evening star's white path
The rising full moon's gold one flows to meet,
Reflecting the sun on the mystery of the unknown
From which stars and the dead arise on night's fountain plume
While the paths exchange colour.

You come when twilight has turned to dark,
The dew and the stars are falling.

Freedom sacred theme that requires the supreme sacrifice,
We shall fly like wild swans on snow wings on the sun path,
Liberty of Divine Creative Love that inspires man.

Buttercup paten,
White moon, communion wafer,
Light the black ocean's silver lily
With the sun's promise of day,
Recalling the dead in the Son
To walk the moonpath to the evening star,
Spiraling golden tower and conch shell castle,
Turning wall smooth as glass, and rose
 That opens door, the listening ear of the sea,
Gabriel shell, bearing the word of God,
"Why don't You come?" hear the Discoverer call,
"Come to me." Silence is the flower of the skull.

Above slow moonlight waves that curl a stair
On Singing Beach, counterpoint,
A rising star sparkles.

Calm or flashing,
Climbing in freedom the dark heights of heaven
While your paths shine on the sea, stars, silent and free;
The aurora borealis rises green and gold phoenix,
Then from the horizon lifts long rays of white and rose
That meeting make a red crown,
Stars shine above in darkness,
While others show through the striped tent
That opens on a halcyon sea's moonpath,
Where the slow shadow of a long wave moving to shore
Silvers a lightning lily.
Eastward under a wide ray of white and rose
The morning star rises red gold from the ocean
Where its path leads to the dawn's regal lily.
Star that glows gold in rose clouds,
Time is visible in your fading.
The moon flies in the long rose wings of dawn's swallow.
Stay for the white swan morning star.

Sunward America my caravel!
Dayspring's discoverer, sails unfurled,
Close hauled, make way from war. Love's compass, God
Pointing Your Peace; Columbus sought the strait
Opening upon the Indies golden roofs,
Pearls for the Queen and infidels for Christ,
Yet found a new world on a favouring wind;
So sail earth's leaning ship to sight New Day.
Blow from wind rose's mouth. Not flies in amber
Encompass, save us; Dawn's Pearl rise Gold Dome.
Enfold world sailing Sonward, Day, Blue Rose.

I wait between the moon and the dawn
Until the rose unfolds through which the sun appearing
Lights the waves' red gold stairs, the sunpath,
That flowing the long tail of the phoenix,
Shines like fire with flames on it,
Orange lilies, martyr stars, spirits;
Ear of corn when grains spire flaming gold angels,
Pointing the way to Christ they compose with the Holy Spirit;
Inspire us to seek while they sing The Ascending;
Between the sun and the moon,
The sun path's sword, changing from gold to white,
Divides the night and day
And shows each final star that floats and spires.

To be woken by the diving of waves in winter
The drop of the comber
The thunder of Michael's armor
Is Paradise moving towards us,
Flying silver walls angels dive over.

Rising wave reveal the sunlight of Your face,
Or shine lightning under white foam,
Or combing thunder Your presence
And pass, messages of fire, foambows.

When Your presence shines in our lives
We are destroyed like the waves.
At best, Your creative need for us,
We have passed
Your most divine message a rainbow host.

Combing from dawn green waves break in shadow;
Fountain regal lilies that each recurve a petal
Seaward to sunrise, gold in their crystal spray.

Oh face the golden folding of excelling splendor,
The rising wave;
Above it the seagull lifting his wings, descending
While it flows from him, the blue smile,
Angel alighting Gabriel
Beyond the closing wave;
And hear the light; advent of waves.
With flaming rainbow hair
Saffire angels stream upon our world
To offer the sun.
See their eyes flash lightning glances
Like the gold leaf of a missal
Or of dew in a field of roses,
The golden flake in snow,
The gold lily in July,
When the Holy Spirit shows the sapphire rose.

v. 2, l. 4, "the blue smile."
"The Cloud," v. 2., l. 7, "Heaven's blue smile."
— Percy B. Shelley, *Poetical Works* (Oxford University Press).

One cold calm winter's dawn
The cove's waves' breath moves
Eastward to the ocean's
Gold rose of mist for sunrise.

On the sand a seagull's feet print a V chalice for the sunpath.
Its ripplemark rim the wavelip rising washes away.

Silence: sapphire: halcyon sea that flows
Ice roses on the snow at Christmastide;
Blue rose so calm the clear waves' lilies
Fold the Sapphire Queen of the sea;
Blue Rose of sunlight seeds, the Universes;
Sea Queen of Sapphire;
Intercede with the Lord of Eternal Life
To inspire man to explore them.

Ocean the light is beyond, sun yet sea
Where sparking snow Michael
Stands on the water assembling stars
That in the rising wave's self-defining shadow
Indicate the breathing heart,
Confluence of stars peerless;
The slow gold root of the reflection rose
Whose silver stems light the cave walls,
Overturning crystal windle,
Sow Your love in the waves of our lives.

Blue rose of the ocean's center
The angels' encircling wings
Your waves stand mountains around a calm
On which moves a single wave
Host of gold stars flashing awns
Ear of wheat
Moving in the wind of the lily
In the long leaves of the swan's wake.

Later Poems

Night silence settles down a calm child's glance.
Only a bird stirs leaves in peace.
How many aeroplanes fly over France?
What battle starts while dawn breaks over Greece?

Black as the faery bluebird
On night's Maylayan tree,
Darkens the heart that sings unheard
Beside the fruit dove sea.

Sun wheeling sapphire wings
The faery bird shines blue.
Dawn love and hear. My whole life sings
And day breaks song in you.

The Blue Rose

The wings of wild winds
Sweep waves in snows and water.
Love is wind, wave, and sea,
The rainbow thrown in spray,
Shadow and light in wave
Rising to curve and break.

Oh restless wind of human hearts,
Love is the mortal water and immortal source.
The soul's tide changes and returns to sea,
The poem and the prayer
To unknown infinite Purpose,
To Eternal Love.
When dawn rises
Grow blue rose.

Autumn

If I could only see
My golden tree.
On the hills the trees tarnish;
The leaves vanish.
In arctic cold
The wood does not turn gold.

Crow caw and cock crow,
Dropping of gold through emerald,
From under water galleon wrecks, October maples,
On All Soul's day the roses smell of apples.

*   *   *

On All Hallow from the maple trees'
Golden aureoles yellow leaves
Like falling stars make carpets for deer
I try to save from shooting.

The Swamp Maple

Coming down the hill it looked as though
My barn were on fire that vandals burnt
Years ago after Halloween,
But it was the swamp maple's leaves
Like flame to glorify God on All Saints' Day
And to remember their sacrifices for freedom,
The green maple by the fire opal
One like the rainbow under blue sky,
A crown of glory.

The falling leaves make the sound of light footsteps
As quietly as forty-five years ago you said
"I am going" and went to war,
And attained your crown of glory.

Autumn [2]

If you sort ash leaves
Remember from which tree they fell,
Or for what tears fall, then tell
Me whom each wind bereaves

Dolferwyn

or

Angels' Meadow

A flock of snowy
Egrets like angels walked with the steers in the meadow.
The pheasant sun rising from the milkweeds
Loosens a silver cloud of silkseeds,
Cherubim,
And lights the frosted pods white flames,
Wings
Of a flock of green and grey birds that clings
To long stems,
Will o' the wisp stars in their beaks;
In goldenrod above the mint near creeks
Milkweed bird ships of seedpeople, Greeks,
Apostles with infants in white silk dresses
Who rise with the sun, a rainbow of angels who fly
From the bows shining stars in blue sky,
Come down silk snow flakes on green grasses.

Dolferwyn

or

Angels' Meadow [2]

A mother holds a child who becoming a kite
Then a star, pulls her and others after him, freed,
A chain of stars floats on air,
Then sailing in sunlight
Each seed
Flies silver wheel of white hair,
Alights an angel in the meadow,
Silk snow.

In a milkweed
Pod
The white seedsilk
Shines like God.

A star Your Hand releases
Departing seed will stand on light,
Silk hair that clings to Your Fingers.
A milkweed sails in calm the evening star.

When sunlight silvers
Their white silk, seeds
In the milkweed's boat
Take flight and float
Like spirits that need
To live forever.

*   *   *

I saw a dun winged angel in the dusk
So weary of sitting on an empty grave
He dozed, half woke, a lyre slipping from
His knees, but only pulled a wing more warmly
In for sleep.
So crowned with roses sank into a well
One who only sat weeping upon
The earth while round her stones
Rose in a circle, wall tower of tears.

The Cherry Tree

When the snow storm ends at Londonderry
Down-Adown-derry in moonlight the cherry,
The poet tree,
Flowers snow stars, poetry,
The sunrise cock pheasant beats off with his wings
Above the snowdrop's bell the cardinal rings.

In April the cherry tree blossoms stars
Where the mourning doves built nests for years
That were robbed till they lay
A V twig on my window sill and flew away
Like black birds with straw beards today.

At night golden lightnings show
The flowering cherry tree in snow.

Who knows if any climber
Clambers from a rose so sweet the umber
Honey dries
The feet of flies
In amber?

The Wood Thrush
La Grieve des Bois

I come to the wood to see the yellow violets,
Then the purple ones the dew shines on at noon,
The jack-in-the-pulpits with shining green curving hoods,
With linings of lightning stripes; wild orchids,
Windflowers, white with pink and silver stripes;
Azaelea bushes, mayflowers, deer,
And on May Day to listen to the thrushes' sweet calls,
Whistles, songs and choir like the Holy Spirit,
Where the dog-wood trees flower like wild swans,
The delicate sweet geraniums are pink and lavender,
The ferns green stars, and later through the wood
Under the trees the Solomon's plumes are white.

The Wood Thrush
La Grieve des Bois [2]

I grieve and fear
That every year
More woods disappear,
Cut down by ruthless men.
In June a terrible west wind
Blew down the northwest end of the wood.
There are no flocks of colored birds here.
Soon I shall be gone.
The moon's white ear
Will shine alone
Above mountains of garbage
Built by totalitarian Americans.

The Hummingbird

The Hummingbird that drinks from the pink rose
Was as green as the fields under the double rainbow.
Between the arc's south ends it was black.

Under the falling stars of the Perseids,
And the white cloud mountains
The field of golden rod flowered
Like galaxies of yellow stars
The butterflies visit,
Until the Mennonite farmer mowed it,
Although I had told him not to.

Meanwhile the totalitarian Americans
Build a mountain of garbage on the south ridge
That pollutes the air and ruins the view,
In the hottest summer on record.

The Great Dipper

In the drought in August I was frightened to see
The green maple trees were yellow
In the rainbow in the sunset,
But they were green again in the morning.

In the evening when the sky was clear and dark
The stars of the Great Dipper came out
In the northwest like a promise of water.
Later beyond it the Hubble space telescope showed
Further into the universe than man had seen,
And the comet Hale-Bopp appeared
After three thousand years.

Christmas

The shepherds in amaze
Saw the star ablaze
And heard the angels praise
The Christ child born in a barn
On Christmas morn.

Valentine's Day

On Valentine's Day the cardinals' flying hearts
Over the snow are seen through the window
That reflects the fire on the hearth.

A Contrast of Ice and Glass

A Contrast of Ice and Glass

Watching the rose clouds before sunrise
Over the snow fields and barns,
The blue jays and cardinals
From the house window I see from the eave
There hangs a long icicle arm,
When the sun shines through its crystal hand
From its lengthening fingers that point down
Water runs,
Oracles when roofs and graves fall in,
A terrible warning of horrible wars.

At Longwood in the glass conservatory in the snow
It is like gardens of spring in winter,
A heaven created by man of real flowers:
Camellia trees, yellow primroses, daffodils, and tulips,
Forget-me-nots with pink amaryllis, and tulips,
Delphiniums, narcissus, foxgloves, and blue daisies,
An acacia walk to the orchids of every color;
The golden slipper, the green ports of Paradise,
The green and white Paphiopedilum,
The red miltonia with the gold angel in the center,
The white orchids with yellow trumpets like angels,
The white orchids with purple on their petals,
The lavender and purple orchids,
Then blue cineraria and yellow tulips.
Outdoors the snow melted one day
And the yellow crocuses appeared
Before the next snow storm.
Inside the conservatory were
The Dutch irises, the Blue Diamonds in yellow sweet broom.

A field of buttercups like those we held
Under each other's chins to see the gold light
On our skin when we were children,
A memory that survives like the buttercups
That after a terrible thunderstorm and heavy rain,
The next morning still lift golden chalices
For sunlight all day and close
Silently before sunset, when the wood thrush
Returned from Mexico singing enchants the place.

The Dance of the Yellow Swallowtail Butterflies

When the white roses flower in the hedges
And climb the trees from which they hang
In long sprays like cascades and fountains,
Where tulip poplar trees flower
Their yellow and orange lamps
The yellow swallowtail butterflies dance
In the secret garden.

July

The Swallow Hill field is extremely hot.
So I climb to the shade of the tulip poplars
That I had planted twenty years ago.
Inside one, under its branches,
A southwest wind cools me.
Outside in the sun on the top of the hill
A black butterfly with yellow spots
Along the outside of its wings, the Black Prince,
Dances back and forth and floats on the breeze
Where ones like him have been for years.
The orange butterfly bushes are empty.
The butterflies must have been stolen.
There is clover for them because I had it planted.
There is still a small one that is bright blue
When its wings are open.
The swallows cross and recross
Me on the path to the garden.
The view of the Doe Run Valley opens
Like a box of emeralds.

September

The goldenrod
Is like the hair of God
Behind the pink rose
The green hummingbird takes nectar from,
Then tries the red bud
And flies to the goldenrod
Where he sits, then flies to the sun
Like the Divine Inspiration
Of the poem he creates.

The Firefly

I woke up at night. I thought I saw
Lightning in the top of a window
And later on the ceiling but there was no thunder.
It was a firefly that first made a very bright light
And then flew across the room, like a comet,
Floating. Then it became dark, and presently
Would light up again and fly across the
Room again. It repeated this several times
Until I wondered if it could set my hair
On fire. Then it became dark.
I opened a window for the firefly to fly out.

The Swamp Maple [2]

When the swamp maple tree is turning
It looks as though the leaves are burning,
Flame the crimson of the Dalai Lama's robe,
Yellow of the monks of Tibet
Destroyed by the crimes of China,
Tree that astonishes in the sun
Vanishes in the wind.

The Valley

The Valley*

My heart, tired of everything, even of hope,
No longer go to importune the fate of your wishes,
Only lend me, valleys of my childhood
A refuge of a day to await death.

See the narrow path of the obscure valley:
From the side of the slopes hang thick woods
That, their intermingled shade, leaning over my forehead
Cover me entirely with silence and peace.

There, two creeks hidden under the bridges of foliage
Trace winding the contours of the valley;
They mingle their wave and their murmur a moment,
And not far from their spring disappear without name.

The spring of my days has run away like them;
It passed without a sound, without name, and without return:
But their wave is clear, and my troubled soul
Will not have reflected the splendor of a fine day.

The freshness of their beds, the shade that crowns them,
Captivates me all day on the banks of the creeks,
Like a child rocked by a monotonous song,
My soul is stilled by the murmur of the waters.

* Translated from the French of Alphonse de Lamartine (1790–1869),
"Le Vallon," published in his 1820 volume, *Meditations*.

Ah. It is there, surrounded by a rampart of foliage
A limited horizon that suffices my eyes
I love to fix my steps and, alone in nature,
Hear nothing but the wave, see nothing but the skies.

I have seen too much, felt too much, loved too much in my life;
I come living to hunt the calm of Lethe.
Beautiful places, be for me the banks where one forgets,
Forgetfulness alone henceforth is my happiness.

My heart is at rest, my soul is in silence.
The distant noise of the world expires while arriving,
Like a distant sound that the distance makes fainter,
Carried by the wind to the uncertain ear.

From here I see life, through a cloud,
Vanish for me in the shadow of the past;
Love alone has remained: as a great image
Survives alone at waking in a dream effaced.

Rest, my soul, in this last refuge,
Like a voyager who, the heart full of hope,
Sits down before entering the doors of the city,
And breathes for a minute the perfumed air.

Like him, shaking the dust from our feet,
Man never passes by this road again.
Like him, at the end of the career we breathe
This calm forerunner of eternal peace.

Index of First Lines

The Blue Rose

3   All the gardens stifle one who looked

4   Before the regal lilies' crown

5   When breathing breaks in the breast

6   O Saviour.

7   On wind-wrought corners of the world

8   Petals cool with dew, the hand that dies,

9   The blue rose of evening darkens rose of night,

Icicle Butterfly Tree

13   The leafless tree

14   An icicle star changing colour stays gold.

15   While mist veils a gold field of wheat

16   Where in green twilights of full moons

17   While a man circling earth in space is the first

18   I would have held You

19   The lost

20   The icicle flames the daffodil

21   Flame the promise of the grain of corn,

22   You of whose existence we know only indirectly,

23   When Orpheus turns around

24   He who in contemplation seeks the truth

25   When dew glitters for joy on the most delicate fern

26 By the clear spring, curled in a veil of dreams,

27 Green wings, a fern star angel bows to the sun

28 Entrance me tree of stars and butterflies,

29 Tree the shape of a lyre, overflow with flowers,

30 Iceberg afire on night's self-questioning seas

31 Our eyes may never hold the sun at noon

32 Crow chanticleer.

33 At the eastern gates

The Egg

37 All the bells

38 Wind-rounded rose buds twined in grapevines

39 What archer stringing sunbeams tries the rainbow?

40 When caught in green ice grotto night's crevasse

The Black Lily

43 We are the martyrs, victims

44 The resurgent dead are shadows,

45 For us there was hardly spring and little that resembled love

46 Why do we dread our form's distortion

47 The poppy flames conceal

48 Frost in moonlight grows the white fern

49 By the dark river in the paling sky

50 Red tree the sun illumines

51 Though hate torture lies can twist all

52 Cross that stars the green grape,

53 Rose, star of evening,

54 Snow crystals grow in clouds,

55 If Green Flake White Lily snowed

56 Who enters darkness, solitude, despair?

57 In the dark garden

58 Why does your candle sing, rainbow the sun

59 Star, cross in darkness unseen,

60 Darling, lift your dark eyes' lashes,

61 Spirit of the gold-winged sandal,

62 When the phoenix turns his emerald head

63 Rose Lily Chalice of Eternal Light,

64 Who are you angel?

65 Brush, push aside

66 No. I am not like the fountain

67 O child seeking the rainbow in the fountain

68 Feel the tension in me as morning. Ask dawn,

69 Glimmering the angel fades and softly
darkness

70 Star cucumber gently sow

The Rainbow Shell

73 When I come to Singing Beach

74 Where several gulls descending lift of wings

75 Wave breaking leaf reverse the scallop's valve,

76 What hand in one turning uncircles

77 Pour steady wind from inland

78 Love's not the last wave's shell.

Singing Beach

81 The seagull's feet print the sand with bows and
    arrows

82 Calm sea-waves slide from the sunpath,

83 I walked behind the inland wind to sea;

84 From the east the mist on the grey ocean

85 Death on the horizon over the ocean;

86 The ocean begins when I come, darkness and
    light,

87 Unroll your royal blue field, ocean,

88 When the green ocean's lilies break in bloom

89 The superb white Paradise mantles his tail.

90 When sunlight beads the sleeves of foam

91 Under the Christmas Eve snow curved

92 Icicles the clairvoyant weep their complicated
    deaths

93 A snow hill point in the ocean is seen

94 By the cradle Saint Michael says to grim
    Grendel:

95 Mounting stars of living waves

96 Speak not of despair;

97 Ocean: blue roller bird:

98 Wave that combing snow cloud stands
    mountain,

The Fountain

101 Once you came walking here between black
      marble columns,
102 O hands that warn and point, create and
      crown;
103 In You the individual is always outside in the
      garden,
104 I have unfolded the tragic rose to you
105 When the self we long to become is the
      sacrifice we may avoid,

The Rose

109 Star of dawn; there was no shade on the road
110 I saw the rose of blood grow darker wine
111 In twilight the crown of crimson roses becomes
      black velvet
112 My rose He gave you to me.
113 When we exhaust ourselves to love those who
      hate us,
114 Stars dawns and roses are Your spirit,

The Alps

117 Eastward on the mountain's crest, dawn snow
118 A swan's wing cloud from the snow mountain
      darkens the lake
119 Serene and beribboned with breezes
120 Son in Your perfect circle at noon

121 White rose,

122 On the green alp in marshmarigolds

123 From the raving noon I entered a wood,

124 Like water that falling curls in wreathes

125 By the clear spring, curled in a veil of dreams

126 Uther Pendragon's Indian of Pennsylvania

127 Above the snow mountain's rose wings

128 Morning star in a rose sky;

129 The snow mountains shining praise You.

130 Give me your love from the remote heavens

131 What drove the poet up the mountainside

132 Clouds; do snow mountains remember or
     dream you

133 Day is dearest blue in the alps

134 O Light that falls through clouds upon far
     snows

135 Withdraw in sapphire, sun, and ray a crown,

136 Peace: snow mountain peaks we longed to
     reach;

137 From the valley where clouds appear

138 We climb to the solitude of the snow mountain
     angels

139 On a mountain top a snow Pegasus lifts cloud
     wings.

140 Creator or destroyer,

141 Under the sapphire skies

142 When rivers of clouds fill the valleys with dreams,

143 At peacock water, in the poplar

The Wheat

147 I cannot walk among the ripening wheat,

148 Always the way fades early.

149 All who listen by windows all night,

150 Thrust freedom's torch down holes where Europe was.

151 The ocean's full moon

152 They dream till fear wakes them in dawns of thrushes

153 When your green hair blows gold from the helm

154 Your intuition of purpose in suffering,

155 I saw the wheat take light upon the slopes of dawn.

156 A wind of swallows waves the sea of wheat,

157 Wheat on a hill doth take the wind

Swallow Hill

161 On the Swallow Hill

162 When Oberon the moon comes up the dark valley

163 Night's wings enclosed the yellow wings of day

164 Cumulus clouds rise Windsor castles,

165 Swallows fly

166 Across a red and white striped field

167 Dansez, dansez papillon noire

168 One August noon a star falling

169 The swallow-tail butterfly suns his open wings

170 In battle, in war the hand of the Lord seized us

171 Red tree the sun illumines

172 When the mist of October mornings,

173 The swamp maple flames like love to remember

174 Like my hope of saving the wood, on Swallow Hill

175 At sunrise in December snow stars

176 The snow winds blow all night.

The Wild Swans in Pennsylvania

179 The glory of woods, tulip poplars yellow,

180 Pure white mitres shake

181 From the organized crime of psychiatry,

182 On the day of the first snow in the meadow

183 The Swan's white feather

The Crimson Crocus

187 Swan of dawn in sapphire thundering

188 Where the beech missal falls

189 As if from our anguish and partings

190 Straight from Christ, feather wet in the crimson muse,

191 Dawn pen the wind moves to write in a green
     star,
192 When the sun melts the stars and opens the
     crocus egg,
193 Adoring stars in luminous blue, the saffrons,
194 The saffron closing the sun in a phoenix egg
195 On the west a line of Himalayan spruces
196 If doomsday dawns, holding the pearl stem
197 Where gentian days arise between the sun and
     the moon,

The Sun Path
201 No day so diamonded or wave can walk from
     light,
202 Serene sea evening Queen
203 Waiting: Columbus on Jamaica's shore,
204 Buttercup paten,
205 Calm or flashing,
206 Sunward America my caravel!
207 I wait between the moon and the dawn
208 To be woken by the diving of waves in winter
209 Combing from dawn green waves break in
     shadow;
210 One cold calm winter's dawn
211 Ocean the light is beyond, sun yet sea

Later Poems

215 Night silence settles down a calm child's glance.

216 Black as the faery bluebird

217 The wings of wild winds

218 If I could only see

219 Crow caw and cock crow,

220 Coming down the hill it looked as though

221 If you sort ash leaves

222 A flock of snowy

223 A mother holds a child who becoming a kite

224 When sunlight silvers

225 When the snow storm ends at Londonderry

226 Who knows if any climber

227 I come to the wood to see the yellow violets,

228 I grieve and fear

229 The Hummingbird that drinks from the pink rose

230 In the drought in August I was frightened to see

231 The shepherds in amaze

232 On Valentine's Day the cardinals' flying hearts

A Contrast of Ice and Glass

235 Watching the rose clouds before sunrise

236 At Longwood in the glass conservatory in the snow

237 A field of buttercups like those we held

256

238 When the white roses flower in the hedges
239 The Swallow Hill field is extremely hot.
240 The goldenrod
241 I woke up at night. I thought I saw
242 When the swamp maple tree is turning

The Valley
245 My heart, tired of everything, even of hope,

List of Poems with Titles

The Swans in Winter   182
The Swan's Feather   183
The Blue Rose   217
Autumn   218
The Swamp Maple   220
Autumn [2]   221
Dolferwyn or Angels' Meadow   222
Dolferwyn or Angels' Meadow [2]   223
The Cherry Tree   225
The Wood Thrush, La Grieve des Bois   227
The Wood Thrush, La Grieve des Bois [2]   228
The Hummingbird   229
The Great Dipper   230
Christmas   231
Valentine's Day   232
A Contrast of Ice and Glass   235
The Dance of the Yellow Swallowtail Butterflies   238
July   239
September   240
The Firefly   241
The Swamp Maple [2]   242
The Valley (translation from Lamartine)   245